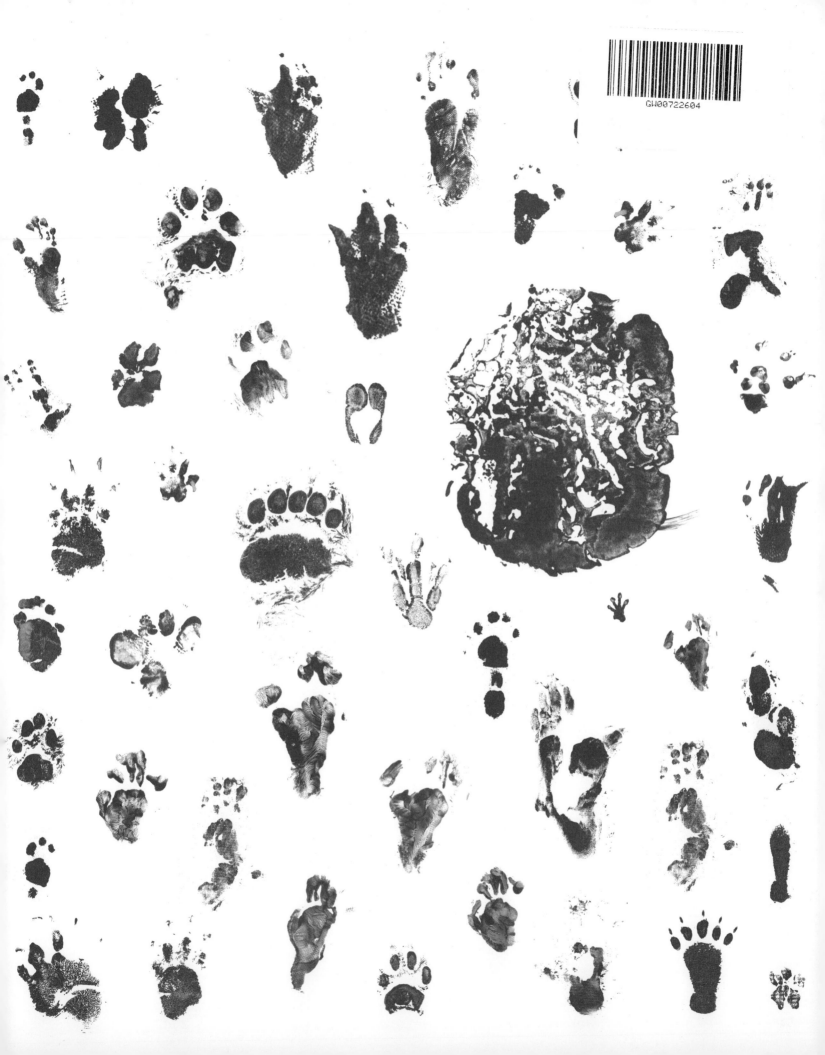

Time at
TARONGA
a zoo down-under

CATHARINE RETTER

citrus press

First published by Citrus Press 2016
PO Box 478, Northbridge NSW 2063 Australia
Text © Catharine Retter
Images © Taronga Conservation Society Australia, unless otherwise credited
Not to be copied whole or in part without written authorisation.
ISBN 978-0-9875095-7-4

Designed by Jude Rowe, Agave Creative Group
Printed in China through Book Production Solutions

AUSTRALASIA

THE AMERICAS

Introduction

Congratulations to Taronga Zoo on putting together such a fine collection of excellent photographs. These images, collectively, show the diversity of the natural world, the amazing variety of life forms with whom we share (or should share) planet Earth. I hope you will pause, as you turn over each page, and spend a few moments with the animal depicted so that you get some sense of its 'being-ness'. And I hope that you will do more than just look through these photos. I hope that you will think about the different animals and feel the need to learn more about those with whom you are least familiar.

Some of them are labelled threatened or endangered. Which means that, unless we humans wake up to all that is going on — as we clear habitats, drain wetlands, pollute the environment, hunt them for their body parts, capture them for exploitation in entertainment and so on — some of them will be known to children of the future ONLY from photos like these.

We are told, again and again, that we are in the midst of the sixth great extinction and as you slowly turn the pages of this book, imagining the long evolutionary process that gave rise to each species, I hope you will get a new sense of the need to work together to slow down and eventually stop this destruction of the natural world.

Tarongo Zoo and the Jane Goodall Institute Australia are collaborating to try to make this a safer world for animals and their environments — and for ourselves as well, for we are all interconnected.

I hope that this book will inspire you to help us.

Dr Jane Goodall, DBE,
Founder —The Jane Goodall Institute
and UN Messenger of Peace.

www.janegoodall.org.au

Chimpanzee, Furahi.

AFRICA

African Lion

It's hard to imagine the extinction of the African Lion (*Panthera leo*) but two sub-species of lion are already extinct. Lions once ranged from northern Africa through southwest Asia (where they disappeared from most Asian countries within the last 150 years), west into Europe (where they are thought to have become extinct almost 2,000 years ago), and east into India.

Today, just two main sub-species remain: the African Lion, and the Asiatic Lion, of which there are only 350 protected animals in the Gir National Park in India. The African Lion is listed as Vulnerable* by the International Union for the Conservation of Nature, with a substantial decline in their numbers outside protected areas over the past three generations.

77 percent of Africa's lion population is found in East and Southern Africa where there is a tourism wildlife infrastructure that supports lions. They live mainly in a number of large and well-managed protected areas, and generate significant revenue for park management and local communities — a strong local incentive to preserve the species.

In West Africa, lions are classified as regionally Endangered*, and they have already been wiped out in North Africa, with the last Numidian Lion shot by a trophy hunter in the 1930s.

RIGHT: The lion is the only truly social big cat, living in prides with a dominant male, four to six related females and their cubs. A male lion's mane is attractive to lionesses as an indicator of good genes, health and nutrition. Its bulk is also suitably intimidating to other males.

LEFT: When they were cubs, Johari and Asali liked to pounce on Jambo's tail as it twitched in the grass, giving a passing headbutt, particularly if he was snoozing, and generally testing his patience.

BELOW: Jambo, known as Bruiser to his keepers, came to the Zoo as a cub in 1999. Kuchani was just a year old when she arrived at Taronga from Auckland Zoo in 2002. They were introduced gradually, with the keepers standing by. Although Kuchani weighed less than half of Jambo, she put on a bold front by swiping aggressively at him when he came too close, earning Jambo's immediate respect.

In 2003, so dramatically had wild populations collapsed that zookeepers across Australia and New Zealand began preparing family trees, and an official 'stud book' was established for the 60 African lions in the region to ensure prides of genetically pure stock could be established in zoos like Taronga. It was no small task to trace the lions back to wild caught populations, but today the most suitable individuals can be chosen to breed, and their offspring sent around the world, to help safeguard a secure population in captivity.

The Taronga Conservation Society Australia also helps to support conservation projects in Africa such as the South Luangwa Conservation Society in Zambia, a project that protects animals and the environments they live in, as well as educating local communities against poaching.

Lions are under threat from habitat loss, illegal hunting, loss of the prey species they feed on, and the impact of feline AIDS. As wild habitats shrink, lion populations also become isolated from each other, cutting access to a wide genetic pool, so zoo populations become increasingly important in maintaining a strong, viable gene pool.

At Taronga, the male, Jambo (his roar can be heard over 8 km away) and female, Kuchani, are descended from a long line of zoo lions. Kuchani came to Australia via South Africa and New Zealand. She has no relatives here, so there is no risk of inbreeding. In 2003, her cubs, Johari (strong) and Asali (honey), became the first to be born at Taronga in 22 years.

* Assessed, 2008

Chimpanzee

In many respects the Chimpanzees (*Pan troglodytes*) at Taronga mirror the ways in which attitudes to wild animals and the role of zoos have changed over the years. And perhaps none more so than long time matriarch, Lulu. Unlike today's chimpanzees at Taronga, she was born in the wild in 1952 and ended up in a circus where she wore a tutu and learnt to ride a bicycle, roller-skate and attend afternoon tea parties. There are tales of her rambunctious behaviour as a teenager, and the circus then wisely decided to transfer her to an American zoo. It was a path that eventually led her to Taronga as a 13 year old.

The zookeepers at Taronga quickly realised they had an intelligent and assertive chimp on their hands, but one that didn't know how to interact with the rest of the group. The chimps at the Zoo interact just like their wild counterparts and have all the social and political complexities that make up wild chimp communities. Lulu was very guarded and possessive about food, and quickly became involved in any disputes. She had to slowly learn how to fit into a community and, eventually, how to be a mother.

Given her start in life, it's a testament to her intelligence that she not only adapted to her new chimp community but rose within their hierarchy to become one of the highest ranking females in the group. That's quite a lofty status when you consider Taronga's chimpanzee family has become recognised internationally as one of the most significant in the world.

Lulu was uncannily perceptive, always very aware of activities on Sydney Harbour which she could see from her high vantage point. And each year, when boats gathered in their thousands for events such as the New Year's Eve fireworks, she seemed to sense that something significant was afoot and remained outside overnight to stay up for the fireworks long after the others had retired to their dens.

RIGHT: Shiba and Sembe

14

Taronga works in partnership with the Jane Goodall Institute to support the Tchimpounga Rehabilitation Centre in the Republic of Congo to release chimpanzees back into the wild. As well as financial support, Taronga sends vets, zookeepers, construction specialists, electricians and volunteers to work at the Centre.

Taronga is also a co-founder of the Chimpanzee Sanctuary and Wildlife Conservation Trust, which manages the Ngamba Island Sanctuary in Lake Victoria, Uganda, housing orphaned chimps saved from poachers and the illegal pet trade.

The Zoo also continues to gather valuable information through its 'Chimpanzoo' program in which Taronga Zoo volunteers regularly monitor the chimpanzees' behaviour to help zoo-based programs and conservation efforts in the wild.

In 1941 at Taronga, long before Lulu, a chimp called Keefi became the first to be born and successfully hand-raised in the Zoo when her mother couldn't care for her. Robert Patten, then superintendent and curator, took her home where she was bottle-fed every six hours for three months. The stove in the loungeroom was kept permanently on, to keep the room at 'jungle' temperature. His meticulous records on her care and progress became a bible for many others around the world and helped the survival of many more chimp babies. When Keefi was at last big enough and healthy enough to make Taronga her home, her keepers were the first female zookeepers at Taronga (a consequence of many of the men being at war).

Another famous, though shorter term resident, at Taronga was Cheeta who starred in the Tarzan movie with Johnny Weismuller. In 1959, a yacht on which he was travelling with his owner (the actor, John Calvert) broke down in the Arafura Sea and was beached on Elcho Island off Arnhem Land. In breach of quarantine laws, Cheeta was in danger of being put down, so the Chairman of the Taronga Trust and benefactor, Sir Edward Hallstrom, chartered a DC3 aeroplane to rescue Cheeta and quarantine him at Taronga. Here they found they had a seven-year-old, beer drinking, chain-smoking, eye-rolling comedian on their hands who could balance a plate with six eggs on his head while chewing mouthfuls of porridge. Cheeta's rehabilitation in quarantine began immediately!

RIGHT: Kamili.

BELOW: Former matriarch, Lulu.

Taronga was one of the first zoos to house and exhibit chimpanzees as a group. When the chimps moved to their new, world-class exhibit in 1981, Dr Jane Goodall gave it her stamp of approval but, more importantly, so did the chimps.

Chimpanzees inhabit forests, woodlands and savannah areas and they are both arboreal and terrestrial, so the new exhibit was structured to echo their natural habitat. Further refurbished in 2011, the exhibit's design was a major team effort by the keepers, vets, exhibit planners, behavioural biologists, and even the volunteers who helped weave a 180 kg hammock from fire hoses for the chimps. There's even a special mesh curtain that divides the interior space so new chimps can be slowly introduced into the group, or to provide family members a space for 'time out' from each other should they need it.

Although they are the most abundant and widespread of the apes, chimpanzees are officially considered Endangered* with an estimated 50 percent reduction in their populations across three generations. Their numbers have declined as a direct result of habitat destruction, poaching and their susceptibility to human diseases, a sad by-product of tourism and their increasing proximity to human populations in Equatorial Africa. Their low rate of reproduction also makes them slow to replace their depleted numbers and, if no action is taken, they will become extinct.

When Lulu passed away at the venerable age of 62, she was not only one of the world's oldest chimps, but left behind a legacy of eight children, six grandchildren and seven great-grandchildren to help the survival of her species. One of her adult sons, Lubutu, became the dominant male of the group in 2001. Even after her child-bearing days, Lulu continued to play an important role in the chimp community, adopting a chimp, Chimbuka, and caring for him after his mother died. She had also demonstrated a wealth of experience in animal behaviour and care that her zookeepers learnt from. Not bad going for a rambunctious misfit with an exploited start in life.

*Assessed by the International Union of Conservation of Nature, 2008.

TOP: Chimps enjoy chilling out and relaxing in the sun as much as their human counterparts.

BOTTOM LEFT: Mother Shiba holds baby Sule.

BOTTOM RIGHT: Sembe devouring a mango. Fruit is an important part of the chimp's diet in the wild.

Fennec Fox

The Fennec Fox (*Vulpes zerda*) is about the size of a Chihuahua and weighs up to 1.5 kg, making it the world's smallest canid. It parades a pair of over-sized ears that look as though they may have been borrowed from a much larger relative.

Fennec Foxes are commonly found in the deserts of Sahara and North Africa, the Sinai Peninsula and into Arabia, where they have developed some remarkable survival adaptations for the hot, dry climate. Their creamy to sandy-yellow coat is designed to blend in with the desert sands and, even at Taronga, they are well camouflaged so that visitors sometimes take a while to pick them out against their desert-scaped exhibit. Fennecs' ears act much like an elephant's, allowing blood vessels close to the skin to dissipate body heat. Their feet are also well adapted to desert living with thick fur between the pads insulating them from the hot sand and muffling their footsteps when stalking prey. They have unusually thick fur for a desert animal but, because they are nocturnal, they need insulation against the cold desert nights. Their long bushy tails (known as 'sweeps') help them change direction when running, as well as warming nose and feet when the fox curls up in its den for the night.

Fennecs burrow interconnected dens at the bottom of stable sand dunes, where moisture and vegetation are more likely to be found. While other foxes are normally solitary, Fennec Foxes forms groups — called a skulk or a leash — and live in a community in the burrows. They rear their young (called 'kits') in tunnels that can be as deep as 4.5 metres below the desert surface.

RIGHT: Taronga's Fennec Foxes love their heat lamp. They begin to shiver when the desert temperature drops below 20°C (68°F) at night, and don't pant until it reaches 35°C (95°F). Ever water conscious, they curl their tongues so that saliva is not wasted when they pant.

Fennecs stalk small birds, lizards and mice with great agility and are able to jump more than half a metre straight up, and more than a metre forwards from a standing position. They can live indefinitely without water, obtaining most of their moisture from grasses, roots, fruits and berries.

So little is known of the Fennec Fox's basic ecology, reproduction and behaviour in the wild, or even accurate population numbers, that zoos play an important role in studying them to improve the world's knowledge of this little-known species. In Australia, the zoo-based population fell as low as six individuals in 2010, so Taronga's breeding program has been important in introducing new bloodlines into the zoo populations.

Taronga's Fennec Foxes have bred successfully a number of times, with their kits growing up to join other breeding programs across Australasian zoos. Taronga's first kits were born to Zinder, a male (called a 'reynard') from Germany, and Kebilli, a vixen from Poland. Fennec Foxes mate for life and, in the wild, live with their offspring in a family unit of up to ten individuals.

The status of Fennec Foxes is listed as being of Least Concern* by the International Union for the Conservation of Nature but with the proviso that detailed information on their abundance is unknown and that new permanent human settlements, such as ones in southern Morocco, have resulted in the disappearance of Fennec Foxes in those areas.

*Assessed 2008

TOP: Young Fennec Foxes, known as a 'kits', are so small, they can fit in the palm of your hand.

BOTTOM: Their large ears help Fennec Foxes hear the smallest of sounds, even beetles and locusts walking along the sand or insects burrowing in the ground.

Giraffe

The Giraffe (*Giraffa camelopardalis*) is the biggest ruminant and the tallest mammal in the world. It is related to other even-toed ungulates, such as deer and cattle, but its closest living relative is the forest-dwelling Okapi (which looks a little like a beautiful mythical beast, a cross between a zebra and a giraffe).

The giraffe's immense height, coupled with its graceful movement and gentle personality gives it the appearance of a gentle giant but, with hooves the size of dinner plates and legs that can be aimed in almost any direction to defend itself, one kick is enough to kill a lion, shattering its skull or breaking the lion's neck.

With the combination of a long neck and long legs, a giraffe's heart must pump blood 2.5 metres up to the brain, and 2.5 metres down when it lowers its head to drink. To avoid a sudden rush of blood to the head and a sudden increase in blood pressure, the giraffe's circulatory system has a valve mechanism to slow the rush of blood back to the heart from the brain.

That's not all that is long about the giraffe. Its tongue can measure up to half a metre in length, which is not only useful for cleaning bugs off its face but also for delicately picking its nose. (Perhaps it's just as well, for no one has ever seen a giraffe bathing in waterholes or swimming in rivers.)

Taronga's Giraffe population helps ensure their long-term viability and continuance for education, exhibit and conservation purposes. The Zoo's successful breeding program has seen 'Taronga' Giraffes sent to New Zealand and other zoos around Australia.

RIGHT: Giraffes have the largest eyes of any land mammal to allow them to see approaching predators up to two kilometres away, keep the rest of the herd in sight and, at Taronga, to admire their unique view.

The first giraffe to arrive in the Australasian region was a wild-caught male, imported in 1926. Taronga then imported several more animals from various parts of Africa in the late 1920s and early 1930s.

To ensure the optimal genetic diversity of giraffes in Australasian zoos, they are managed at the species level. While different sub-species are identified, the Australasian Species Management Plan deliberately aims to keep the overall population as genetically diverse as possible.

Authorities differ on the number of sub-species of giraffe that exist (anything from five to 12), identified by their geographic range, coat pattern and coat colouring. The exact pattern is as unique to each individual as a fingerprint.

The more genetic variation that is retained in zoo populations, the greater their potential to serve as a viable reservoir in the event that wild populations suffer a dramatic collapse.

While giraffes, over all, are not a threatened species, populations are vulnerable in many localities. The conservation status of wild giraffes is listed as low risk but conservation dependant.

TOP: Taronga's giraffes savour the rain on their tongues — easier than bending 2.5 metres down to the ground to drink.

FAR LEFT: When feeding, the giraffe carefully curls its tongue around leaves, shoots and buds, many of which can have long, sharp thorns. It can then deftly strip off any remaining twigs with a backward pull of its head. The distinctive blue or blue–black of a giraffe's tongue acts like a sunscreen, and its colouring is caused by very few blood vessels. It's nature's way of ensuring the tongue bleeds less from the prickly vegetation the giraffe feeds on.

LEFT: The cartilage horns, more correctly known as ossicones, are covered with skin and have a tuft of hair at the tip. They are one of the few ruminants born with horns which — very considerately for mum — lie flat during birth. For an older bull, the horns add weight to his head, and therefore greater impact when he swings his neck to fight a rival.

Some efforts to reintroduce individuals back into protected areas have proven successful but their populations remain fragmented. Their numbers are increasing in southern African but northern populations have been less fortunate as a result of habitat degradation and poaching and, in some parts of their traditional range, they have become locally extinct. Overall Giraffe numbers are estimated at around 80,000 (dropping from 140,000 in 1999) and their long-term future is of considerable concern.

*Assessed by International Union for Conservation of Nature 2010

RIGHT: Despite its great length, the giraffe's neck has the same number of vertebrae as a human neck (seven), but it makes up the difference with very large, elongated bones. The bulls, in particular, use their two-metre necks and antler-like horns to joust with rivals, striking at each other's necks, underbellies and flanks. The fights can result in broken jaws, necks, or even knocking the other unconscious.

Pygmy Hippopotamus

If you happen to walk by the Pygmy Hippopotamus (*Choeropsis liberiensis*) exhibit at Taronga and hear a cacophony of honking and snorting, you can assume love is in the air. Taronga's zookeepers are counting on potential suitor, Fergus, to let them know when Kambiri, his next door neighbour, is ready to be wooed.

Pygmy hippos are usually shy and solitary animals so they need to be introduced slowly and from a distance. When Kambiri comes into season, the two will be united for a whirlwind romance — if honking and snorting can be considered romantic.

The reclusive pygmy hippos are seldom seen in the wild and were only discovered in West Africa's swamps and forests in the mid 1800s. Hippopotami (from the Greek for 'river horse') were once believed to be most closely related to pigs until recent genetic studies revealed that their closest living relatives are, in fact, whales! Weighing in at about 250 kg, they are much less sociable than the larger Common Hippopotamus but also less aggressive, and only one-fifth its size.

Pygmy hippos are difficult to observe in their solitary, nocturnal, forest-dwelling lifestyle, so Taronga's experiences have contributed valuable information on their breeding and care to the world's research databank on this species.

Pygmy hippos spend most of the day resting in swamps, wallows, or in hollows alongside streams and rivers. They secrete 'blood-sweat', a thick, oily, white or pinkish built-in antiseptic and sunscreen that protects their skin in the water as well as during dry spells on land. It's what gives hippos their slick, wet look.

RIGHT: Pygmy hippo mum, Petre, displays her formidable tusks. Often she will only need to 'yawn' at potential enemies to scare them off. But if that doesn't work she may rear up, lunge, scoop water with her mouth and shake her head to send them scurrying.

ABOVE: When she was born, piglet-sized Kambiri had yet to perfect the art of swimming, but quickly became a water baby, spending her days bobbing up and down in her waterhole with mum, only coming out when it was time to eat. Soon, she was even able to show off with exuberant somersaults in the water.

RIGHT: Unlike the larger, Common Hippopotamus which has webbed feet, pygmy hippos have well-separated toes with sharp nails.

In the late afternoon and at night, they travel along a regular network of paths that they maintain through the thick vegetation, feeding on ferns, broad-leaved plants, tender shoots and fallen fruit. To reach higher tree branches they stand on their hind legs and balance themselves against a tree with their front legs, looking a little like tubby ballerinas.

The species has only a patchy distribution in Western Africa with an estimated 3,000 left in the wild, mainly in Liberia but also across that country's borders into Sierra Leone, the Ivory Coast and Guinea. Over the next 20 years, their numbers are expected to decline to fewer than 2,500, with the main threat to their existence being habitat loss as forests are logged and converted to farmland. They are also vulnerable to poaching, hunting, natural predators and wars, and have been upgraded from Vulnerable to Endangered status by the International Union for Conservation of Nature*.

Kambiri, whose Nigerian name means 'Allow me to join this family', was only the fifth pygmy hippo born in Australia in two decades (in 2010) and was Taronga's second female calf born to mum, Petre and dad, Timmy. The zookeepers had built such a good relationship with Petre that they were able to conduct ultrasounds throughout the pregnancy, helping them to closely monitor the progress of the foetus.

As baby Kambiri gained in strength and confidence, she showed a stubborn independent streak, refusing to get out of the moat when it was time to head into the night den and, like many toddlers, ignoring her mother by cheekily swimming away when Petre wanted her to come inside.

In the wild, Kambiri would have started to venture out and forage with mum, learning which foods were good to eat and which ones to avoid. At Taronga, watermelon, eaten in big noisy, juicy chunks became a favourite summer treat, but dairy cubes were her favourite — specialised pellets that contain important vitamins and nutrients to ensure she grew up strong and healthy.

Kambiri stayed close to mum until she was around 12 to 18 months of age when it was time for her to go off on her own. By then, sporting a little round hippo belly, she had grown into a very confident and curious young female. Because pygmy hippos are solitary animals, Kambiri time-shares the African Waterhole exhibit in turn with Taronga's other hippos, and has a separate den, complete with her own beauty regime of a misting machine to keep her skin hydrated.

With Foot and Mouth Disease in European countries placing restrictions on the movement of hoofed species, every birth is significant for the local gene pool and Kambiri's ability to produce offspring is a vital addition to Australia's population of pygmy hippos.

*Assessed 2008.

LEFT: The common hippo's teeth and tusks continue to grow throughout life and act as formidable fighting tools in the wild, just as those of the pygmy hippo.

RIGHT TOP: Kambiri made her public debut at Taronga at one month of age, keeping close to mum, Petre.

RIGHT BOTTOM: Under water, hippos instinctively close their ears and noses.

Ring-tailed Lemur

The Ring-tailed Lemur (*Lemur catta*) is a primate, just one of 103 species of lemur. It is relatively large for a lemur and is found only on Madagascar, off the east coast of Africa.

The lemur's startled gaze, ghostly reflective eyes and haunting cries led some Malagasy people to believe that the animals embodied the souls of their ancestors. In Roman mythology 'lemures' referred to the spirits of the dead and although the name 'lemur' was originally selected by naturalists for a different animal in India, it was later redirected, perhaps more appropriately, to the Madagascan animal.

The species name, '*catta*', refers to the lemur's cat-like appearance. It also sounds like a cat from time to time, purring when it is groomed, and meowing to make contact with another — as well as barking, howling, mewing, screaming, and clicking or chirping.

Over 90 percent of lemur species are under threat. Madagascar's forests are the only place these lemurs exist in the wild, and the forests are being burnt for charcoal production, and cleared at an alarming rate for agriculture and settlements. It is estimated that their numbers have decreased by 50 percent in just three generations and, in 2014, the Ring-tailed Lemur was upgraded to Endangered* status by the International Union for Conservation of Nature.

Taronga has established a state-of-the art Lemur Forest that includes more than 5,000 trees and plants. The Zoo has also teamed up with leading Madagascan conservationists to help protect and regenerate their forests, so that animals like the lemur can survive and thrive once more.

RIGHT: The Ring-tailed Lemur's tail is longer than its body and is not prehensile like a monkey's. Other than waving it in 'stink' competitions, the tail is used only for balance, communication, and as a wrap-around body warmer.

Ring-tailed Lemurs are highly social and live in groups, known as 'troops', of up to 30 animals. A dominant female presides over all. The males perform a unique scent-marking behaviour called 'spur marking' and, during mating season, will battle for dominance by trying to out-stink each other. They cover their long tails with smelly secretions and wave them about to determine which is the most powerful to win the right to mate with the dominant female.

Lemurs eat fruits that grow in the forest and play an important role in dispersing the seeds as they pass through the lemurs' bodies. If these lemurs are lost, the entire ecosystem is affected.

*Assessed 2012

RIGHT: Lemurs wake before dawn and move away from their sleeping tree to begin feeding and sunning themselves. During this time they sit upright on their haunches, spread-eagle, exposing their underside, with their thinner white fur towards the sun.

BELOW: Lemurs reaffirm their social bonds by huddling together and mutually grooming. One will present itself to a partner who responds by grasping its fur and licking it or scraping with a tooth. They are also very playful, wrestling and chasing each other around in circles.

Slender-tailed Meerkat

The gregarious Slender-tailed Meerkats (*Suricata suricatta*) are usually seen in groups, with several families living together in a large community. They love grooming one another, wrestling and playing together. They are playfully curious and can make a toy of almost anything.

They might look small and cute but they are cousins to the mongoose and have the ability to kill a cobra, mobbing together to relentlessly attack a snake if it tries to enter their burrow. They are also immune to many venomous animals such as snakes, millipedes and even scorpions, one of their favourite foods.

Meerkats live in the southern region of Africa, an area dominated by the Kalahari Desert. In these areas the daily temperature can vary between as much as 43°C in summer and 18°C in winter, but in the burrows the temperature can range by as little as only one degree.

Slender-tailed Meerkats are carnivores, spending most of their time digging and foraging for insect larvae, moths, butterflies, termites, crickets, spiders, and scorpions which they disarm by biting off the stinging tail. They also eat lizards and birds, as well as fruit. When hunting small game, Meerkats work together, communicating with purring sounds. They will only forage for food during the day and, with safety in numbers, are careful not to lose sight of each other. For the same reason, individuals do not venture out at night for bathroom breaks, preferring to soil their burrow and allowing beetles to clean up the mess when they — understandably — move on to their next burrow.

The meerkat is officially listed as having no major threats to its survival and the role of zoos like Taronga is in educating visitors on the importance of the species and its habitat. They have a wide distribution, and large populations are protected in several well-managed, protected areas.

RIGHT: Malawi with her pups watch out for predators by standing on their hind legs and sometimes bobbing up and down. Although they have excellent distance sight, bobbing up and down changes their visual focal points and is thought to help them get a better perspective on a predator closing in on them.

While the majority of the group is looking for food, a few will always stand guard on their hind legs, watching for predators, particularly birds of prey that can snatch a Meerkat off the ground. When everything looks safe, the sentries send out mellow tones. When a sentry spots a predator in the distance, it quickly makes a more urgent beeping sound. The large Martial eagle tends to generate the most frantic alarm even when still a great distance away.

At Taronga, a sea hawk or pelican flying overhead triggers an alarm, as can a Qantas jet flying overhead for a landing at Mascot Airport. A sharp, shrill call is the signal for all to take cover.

Mating in the gang is reserved for the alpha male and alpha female. Meerkats work their way to this top position through their interactions with the others in the group. Simple behaviours such as taking the best food or the best spot for sunning is how they move up the ranks to become the leader, a process that can often result in small scuffles or jostling until members of the group learn to give way in the new hierarchy. If they don't defer, fights can become vicious and heated. Female meerkats have much higher levels of aggression than males, probably because they invest so much in their producing young, and therefore the right to breed and succeed is well worth their effort.

In 2009, at Taronga's Meerkat Desert, a degree of jostling and posturing was going on during a period when there was no clear leader. During this time, one of the posturing — and pregnant — females, Malawi, produced pups, and it wasn't too long afterwards that her rival, Sahara, succeeded in claiming the top position. The males wisely kept their noses out of the power struggle between the two females.

One of the pups born that year, Nairobi, started to assert her position from the early age of three and was able to achieve a relatively peaceful change to become the next alpha female. In 2015 she was introduced to the brothers Maputo and Xhosa, from Perth Zoo, to form a new breeding group.

TOP: Meerkats have dark 'sunglasses' patches around their eyes, which lessen any glare from the sun. It lets them look directly into the glare and still see a predatory bird approaching. Their ears are adapted to desert life too and can close in the event of a sandstorm or when burrowing.

LEFT: Studies have shown that the pup that begs the loudest gets the most food from the adults.

BELOW: Given half a chance, Meerkats will use any available burrow at the first hint of danger.

Western Lowland Gorilla

The Western Lowland Gorilla (*Gorilla gorilla*) is the most numerous and widespread of all the Gorilla subspecies, so when you hear that it is Critically Endangered* — just one step away from extinction — you realise how dire the gorillas' overall survival is and how precious zoo populations are to their future.

Taronga's first gorilla arrived to much excitement in 1959. With a touch of showmanship, the adult male was named 'King Kong'. He came from the estate of the famous Trader Horn — African adventurer, ivory trader, author — and had been raised as a personal pet, trained to eat steaks and three veg at the table and to drink tea and coffee, until he became too big and powerful and tended to forget his table manners. Record numbers flocked to the Zoo to see King Kong, perhaps with visions of a huge, destructive and lustful beast similar to the star of the popular movie of the same name. At the time of his arrival there were only 40 gorillas in captivity around the world. Six more gorillas came to Taronga in the 1960s, thought to be the largest number in any zoo at that time. They were the stars of Taronga.

Taronga is a partner in the increasingly vital global breeding program, an insurance against a further catastrophic decline in the wild. Taronga and other Australian zoos are also actively encouraging visitors to recycle their old mobile phones to reduce the demand for coltan mining in the gorillas' habitat.

RIGHT: Mother love: Taronga born Mbeli with baby Mjukuu ('grandchild' or 'second generation' in Swahili). He is the first sired by Kibali, Taronga's silverback, and begins the second generation of Western Lowland Gorillas successfully bred at Taronga.

LEFT: Mbeli and Fataki

BELOW: Chillin' out at Taronga.

In 2012, there was a changing of the guard at the Zoo when Kibabu retired as the prime silverback after having sired an impressive 14 offspring over his 36 years. His progeny now live in gorilla communities around the world, from Melbourne to Japan and Europe, where each of them plays a vital role in the European Species Management Breeding Program.

In the wild, a younger male would already have challenged Kibabu for the prime role, potentially resulting in serious injury or death for one of them. Female gorillas also tend to squabble over access to the silverback and it is the silverback's sometimes stressful job to keep the peace within the group. For Kibabu, a quiet retirement with a few favoured females on the NSW South Coast, may have well been a welcome relief for him.

New males who challenge an alpha male are apt to be cowed by intentionally intimidating shows of physical power. The older male will stand to his full height, throw things, make aggressive charges, and pound his huge chest while barking out powerful hoots or unleashing a frightening roar. Despite these displays and the gorillas' obvious physical power, they are generally calm and non-aggressive unless disturbed.

The quest for a new silverback began with Zoo experts working through the International Studbook database using complex software to identify males with the right mix of genetic and temperamental requirements. They measured relatedness, not only to the rest of Taronga's gorilla population, but also to any other gorillas in Australian zoos. The result was an international shortlist of just five males, each of whom was visited by Taronga staff. After the success of silverback, Kibabu, Taronga particularly wanted a male who had also grown up in a family situation, had seen females give birth and who had a strong silverback father from whom he would have learnt good leadership traits and a sense of fairness.

Kibali, a handsome bachelor with a calm and gentle nature appeared to be the perfect match for Taronga's females. Still a blackback, then aged 11 and maturing rapidly into a silverback, he came to Taronga from a French zoo. He was at an age where, in the wild, he would naturally leave his family group to find his own mate and, in this way, Taronga was able to mimic the natural rites of passage for the species.

After quarantine, Kibali was introduced to an adolescent female, 7-year-old Kimya ('Quiet One' in Swahili). She was a good initial match for him in terms of age and temperament, but she rejected his overtures, so he wooed her with gentleness and food offerings. It was a sure-fire strategy to win any girl, and Taronga staff knew they had chosen the right silverback.

More females were introduced into Kibali's group soon after his arrival, among them Mbeli, who was born at Taronga in 2003 and is the daughter of the previous silverback Kibabu. (Mbeli is named after a large swampy clearing that is the focus of a long-term gorilla conservation research project in Africa.) To avoid in-breeding, Mbeli had spent the past few years in Melbourne Zoo and returned to Taronga with another gorilla, Johari, who was born at Melbourne Zoo. Both females are destined to play their part in the regional breeding program for Western Lowland Gorillas.

While introductions to the three females have gone very well, Mbeli in particular remains fascinated by Kibali, and keepers have marvelled that they spend most of their time together. In late 2014, Mbeli gave birth to their son Mjukuu. First-time mum Mbeli had been mother-reared herself, and knew exactly how to care for her tiny baby.

RIGHT: Taronga's silverback, Kibali, arrived from France in 2013.

In the wild, the Western Lowland Gorillas live in a small area of West Africa in dense lowland tropical forests and in swamp forests where their population has declined by more than 80 percent in just over three generations. Their habitat is being criss-crossed and destroyed by logging and coltan mining. Gorilla bushmeat trade is also a major threat, with logging vehicles known to transport the bushmeat, and with logging employees consuming more bushmeat than local villagers. Poaching is a serious problem in even the most protected areas and almost half of the gorillas' protected habitat has also been hard-hit by Ebola virus — including the second largest protected population at Minkébé — with a devastating death rate of over 90 percent. Even if all the threats to Western Lowland Gorillas were miraculously removed, scientists optimistically calculate that the species would require around 75 years to recover.

*Assessed by the International Union for Conservation of Nature, 2008

DNA analysis indicates that Gorillas and Chimpanzees are more closely related to humans than they are to Orang-utans. Like humans, they even giggle when amused. Through inter-zoo breeding, education, and conservation programs, genetically healthy populations are being bred in the hope of saving this important and Critically Endangered primate.

ASIA

Asian Elephant

We're all so used to seeing elephants in documentaries and in zoos that it can be difficult to realise that the Asian Elephant (*Elephas maximus*) is listed as Endangered* by the International Union for the Conservation of Nature's Red List of Threatened Animals. In Thailand, where Taronga's Asian Elephants originated, there are only between 2,500 and 3,200 left, and their population has reduced by at least 50 percent over the last three generations.

Taronga has a long association with Asian Elephants, the first of whom, Jessie, was brought across Sydney Harbour on a barge from the Zoo's original Moore Park site in 1916. In an era when zoos still considered it acceptable to give elephant rides to the public, Jessie regularly strolled through the Zoo with visitors aloft. She lived until 1939, achieving the record for the longest living elephant in captivity.

Today, the emphasis is on elephants living in cohesive matriarchal herds that closely echo the way they would live in the wild, usually with the oldest female acting as the leader. At Taronga, although the elephants are unrelated and came from different places in Thailand, by working together with their experienced keepers, they developed social ties and a herd structure similar to the wild. Pak Boon (Thai for the 'Morning Glory' flower, born in 1992) occupies a high position in the herd, particularly after the birth of her female calf Tukta ('Doll') in 2010.

The Asian Elephant conservation and breeding program for the Australasian region, driven by Taronga's experts and partner zoos, is a vital part of the international efforts designed to ensure a genetically strong and healthy population, to build a self-sustaining population of Asian Elephants in Australia, and to generate funds and other resources for conservation in the wild.

RIGHT: Elephants communicate through touch, smell and taste, and a favourite greeting is to combine all three with a friendly outstretched trunk.

Pak Boon has been ably assisted by another member of the herd, the younger female Tang Mo ('Watermelon' in Thai). Tang Mo has taken the role of esteemed aunty in the social structure, interacting with Tukta and other calves, caring for and protecting them, and standing guard if there are new noises or sights to assess. Both adult females have formed close relationships with their keepers. Pak Boon is something of a tomboy. She is garrulous and energetic and enjoys her daily wash-downs. Tang Mo enjoys challenges and seems to love nothing better than pitting her skills in training exercises. She has a strong bond with the keepers and usually gives a low rumble of pleasure when they arrive each morning to start the day.

Males leave their herd at puberty and Taronga's bull elephant, Gung, moved into his own custom-built accommodation at around the time the females would have sent him on his way in the wild. Gung ('Prawn' in Thai) is very much a boy and behaves exactly as a sexually mature young male elephant should in the wild. He is confident and strong, energetic, exuberant and loud.

His bachelor pad comes complete with a sand pit, heaters and showers, yards with sleeping mounds, a mud wallow and pools with water jets, as well as CCTV coverage — and, importantly, accommodation for up to two visiting females at any time.
Gung and the females communicate across their separate exhibits via rumbles, growls, bellows, and moans. Some of these are low-frequency infrasounds, inaudible to humans, and may travel over long distances to alert another elephant who may chance to be in suburban Sydney.

Of the initial herd members that arrived in Australia, some have now gone to start a separate herd at Taronga's sister zoo in Dubbo, Taronga Western Plains Zoo. Among them is Thong Dee ('Golden' in Thai), a former Bangkok street elephant, who is now an experienced mother to Luk Chai ('Son'), the first calf born into the breeding program in 2009. The gentle and loyal Porntip ('Gift from Heaven') has also accompanied her calf, Pathi Harn ('Miracle') — so named after he was thought to have perished during the protracted labour at his birth. He not only survived against all odds but thrived.

LEFT AND BELOW: Playtime is all about jumbo-sized dips in the pool, rolling, dust baths and playing or picking up objects with their trunks — or in the case of the calves, Luk Chai and Pathi Harn, launching their whole bodies at objects, or each other.

Asian Elephants live in some of the most densely human-populated regions of the world, and habitat loss and competition for feed in farming lands is a major factor in their declining numbers. During the last decade, over 1,300 wild elephants have been killed in Sri Lanka alone from human–elephant conflict resulting in gunshot wounds, poisoning, electrocution, land mines and collisions with vehicles and trains.

Among the many conservation programs Taronga supports, the Zoo provides funding to care for calves at the Elephant Transit Home in Sri Lanka, which has successfully rehabilitated and released over 60 juvenile elephants into the Udawalawe National Park since 1995.

Taronga also supports Thailand's conservation efforts in Kui Buri National Park, including the reduction of human-elephant conflict, and stopping the illegal killing of wild Asian Elephants.

In Sumatra, the Zoo has provided funding to fill in old wells in Way Kambas National Park which have trapped and killed around 300 elephants — as well as Sumatran Tigers and Sumatran Rhinoceros — since 1984.

Taronga has a long history of providing funds, initiatives and expertise for conservation, environmental education, wildlife health, and facility design, as well as management of elephant populations in Thailand, Cambodia, Nepal and Sri Lanka to help protect this Endangered* and much loved species.

*Assessed 2008 by the International Union for Conservation of Nature.

TOP LEFT: Male elephant, Gung demonstrates his tusks. Female Asian Elephants, either do not grow visible tusks, or only small ones, called tushes.
TOP RIGHT: Luk Chai, Tukta and Pathi Harn under the watchful care of Portnip and Pak Boon.
BOTTOM: An elephant's trunk has more than 40,000 muscles, more than all the muscles in a human body. At first a calf may only be able to wave its trunk around in the air, suck on it, or trip over it. The finger-like upper tip of the trunk is so dextrous that eventually it will become adept enough to tear down a tree or pick up a blade of grass. A trunk also comes in handy for snorkelling in the pool.

Asian Small-clawed Otter

The Asian or Oriental Small-clawed Otter (*Aonyx cinerea*) is a member of the weasel family, and the smallest of the world's 13 otter species. It is superbly adapted to aquatic life in freshwater and peat swamp forests, coastal wetlands, and along the banks of paddy fields, lakes and streams. Their very flexible backbone also gives them an acrobatic agility in the water, making them a crowd favourite at the Zoo.

Otters are very intelligent and social animals and, in parts of India, China and Southeast Asia, they are trained to catch fish and return them to the fishing boats in exchange for rewards. At Taronga, the zookeepers are constantly challenged to find new ways to keep the otters stimulated, active and content.

Otters have a very high metabolism and in the wild spend a great portion of their day searching for food, so they are fed eight times a day at the Zoo with feeding sessions made stimulating and complex so they have to work at finding and accessing their food as they would in the wild.

Asian Small-clawed Otters are affected by pollution in waterways, such as pesticide run-off from farmlands. Water pollution and overfishing also reduce the availability of their food sources. Taronga works to educate the community on conserving the environment, including the otter's freshwater habitat.

RIGHT: Escape artist, Houdini, and brother, Soa, are well adapted to aquatic life with long, streamlined bodies, short limbs, webbed feet, waterproof fur and tapering tails.

Otters are listed as Vulnerable* and are poached for their lush fur, but the biggest threat to their survival is habitat loss.

Taronga's otter pair arrived in late 2014 — the female Pia from Melbourne Zoo, and young male Ketut from Perth Zoo — to start a new breeding group at Taronga. After a carefully managed introduction, the two are flourishing, and the Zoo has high hopes for their future breeding success. Otters are very social animals and don't like to be alone, sometimes living in groups of up to 20 members. Pia and Ketut happily spend all their time together at the Zoo.

RIGHT: One of Bising's favourite activities is to slide down the otters' waterfall to ambush her brothers swimming below.

LEFT TOP: The Asian Small-clawed Otter has moist skin on its nose, called the rhinarium, which it uses to detect the direction of scent-bearing winds. It is hand-oriented, meaning it reaches with an outstretched forepaw to search for prey by touch alone.

LEFT BOTTOM: In the wild, the Small-clawed Otter feeds mainly on crabs, snails and other molluscs, insects and small fish but can supplement its diet with rodents, snakes and amphibians too. It has two large crab-crushing teeth making it well-adapted to feed on invertebrates.

Binturong

If there is the smell of burnt popcorn in the air, and perhaps a hint of corn chips, Zoo visitors may think they are nearing the food court but, chances are, it's coming from the Binturong family enclosure. One of the ways Binturongs communicate and mark their territory is through their tails, emitting a strong odour surprisingly similar to these snack foods.

The tree-dwelling Binturong (*Arctictis binturong*) or Asian 'bear-cat' has something of an identity crisis. It is more of a civet than a bear, and is related to meerkats and mongooses. In Malacca it's called a *binturong*, in Malaysia a *benturung*, and in Indonesia a *tenturun*.

It is mainly active at night and, during the day likes nothing better than sunning itself along a branch, lying sprawled out on its stomach with all four legs dangling down. Only its tail tethers it to a branch.

The Binturong is a gentle climber, never leaping from branch to branch, often pausing, climbing slowly and easily along the upper side of branches or along the underside with its prehensile tail acting as a secure anchor. The tail is almost as long as the Binturong's body, and a leathery patch on the underside provides extra non-slip grip. When they descend to move to another tree, you'll see them go down head first, gripping with their sharp, curved claws and using the tail as a brake.

Although Taronga has displayed Binturongs since the late 1950s, breeding them has not been easy and it was not until 2007 that the first Binturong was born at the Zoo. With their numbers in the wild declining by more than 30 percent in just three generations, Taronga's Binturongs are an important source of genetic diversity essential for their long-term conservation.

RIGHT: The Binturong feeds on fruits and small prey like insects, birds and rodents, as well as fish and birds' eggs. It passes undigested seeds throughout the forest and plays an important role in maintaining plant diversity.

Although remaining Binturong populations are widely dispersed across south and southeast Asia, they are now uncommon, even rare, as forests make way for palm oil plantations. They are hunted for the illegal pet trade and, unfortunately, locals consider their flesh a delicacy as well as having medicinal properties. Their rapidly declining numbers have seen the Binturong listed as Vulnerable by the International Union for Conservation of Nature*, and Taronga is a partner in a regional campaign encouraging households and companies to buy only Certified Sustainable Palm Oil.

*Assessed 2008.

ABOVE: Even though little is known about Binturong litters in the wild, Pepper, at 19 years of age, is the oldest Binturong Taronga has had, so it's likely that Indah will be Pepper's last cub, making her very special for her species.

LEFT: Indah, which means 'Beautiful' in Malay, was the first Binturong cub born at Taronga.

Fishing Cat

Fishing Cats (*Prionailurus viverrinus*) evolved from Leopard Cats around six million years ago and, like most cats, are solitary in the wild. They are about twice the size of a domestic cat but, from that point, the differences between them become more obvious. The Fishing Cat, as its name implies, is very comfortable swimming and hunting in the water and has adapted to a wetlands habitat in and around slow-moving water: shallow pools, marshes, mangroves and densely vegetated areas along lakes, reed beds, tidal creeks and rivers.

It is a strong and eager swimmer — sometimes for quite long distances — and uses its short, flattened tail a little like a rudder. It has a very short and dense undercoat to keep its skin warm and relatively dry in the water, and longer 'guard hairs' that give the cat its olive–grey camouflage colours. Its partially webbed toes and semi-retractable claws help in its watery habitat, and its closer-set eyes allow it to focus on fish in the water.

Special conservation efforts are urgently needed to protect the species. Taronga is working with Himalayan Nature to protect key habitats in Nepal, and to establish priority conservation areas in Koshi Tappu Wildlife Reserve, a Ramsar wetland in southern Nepal.

Villagers are being engaged to protect the Fishing Cats as well as the aquatic environment, which in turn benefits local communities by increasing harvestable fish populations and ecotourism.

RIGHT: Fishing Cats communicate with hisses, guttural growls and even the low, demanding meow that is familiar to domestic cat owners. As part of a courtship ritual, the cats make a chittering sound to each other.

The Fishing Cat has adapted its hunting behaviour superbly to its watery environment and will dive from a riverbank onto fish or other small aquatic animals such as frogs, waterfowl and crayfish, using its claws to grab its prey. It has been observed swimming stealthily underwater to catch unsuspecting aquatic birds from below, and even diving from overhanging trees into the water to pounce on prey. Evolution seems to have gone only so far for this cat though, for its small teeth are not ideally designed for holding onto its slippery supper in the water.

As an important predator in its habitat, the Fishing Cat is vital to maintaining a healthy ecosystem, but there has been a 50 percent decline in their population in just three generations. Aquatic pollution, and the need for new farmlands to service ever-increasing human populations, mean traditional habitat protection has not been successful in halting the loss and deterioration of wetlands.

The Fishing Cat has now been listed as Endangered by the International Union for Conservation of Animals* with a further 50 percent loss projected over the next three generations if its habitats cannot be protected.

*Assessed 2010

TOP: One of Cantik's favourite hunting tricks is to lightly tap the surface of the water mimicking the vibrations of insects to attract fish. In the wild, as a fish swims up to investigate, she would scoop her prey up with her paws or, if it is just out of reach, will jump into the water to grab her catch of the day.

BOTTOM: Fishing Cats are primarily nocturnal and, although fish make up the bulk of their diet, they are also known to hunt land animals such as birds, small mammals, snakes and snails. It is hoped the diversity of their diet is something that may help delay their extinction where wetlands give way to farming.

Francois' Leaf-monkey

The Francois' Leaf-monkey, also known as the Francois' Langur (*Trachypithecus francoisi*), is one of the world's rarest monkeys. A handsomely white-sideburned monkey with black silky body hair, it gets its name from its diet of mainly leaves. But just to complicate matters, it also eats flowers, fruit, shoots and bark, and needs a highly specialised stomach divided into four chambers to allow it to digest this tough high-fibre, low protein diet.

Leaf-monkeys live in the canopy of dense forests, and shelter from the weather or seek refuge at night in limestone caves and rock overhangs in cliff faces. They are very agile, in spite of their bulging stomachs caused by their slow-to-digest food.

At Taronga, as in the wild, the adult male, Hanoi, lives with a harem of females and, perhaps because he is spoilt for choice, it's usually the females who will initiate sexual behaviour. Although Hanoi prefers to avoid being a hands-on dad, he will respond to his offspring's distress calls to protect them from harm.

Taronga is one of the few zoos in the world to have successfully bred Leaf-monkeys and is working with other zoos globally to help ensure a future for this species. The aim is to establish an insurance population under the Species Survival Program. Taronga is also involved in conservation projects in North Vietnam.

Saigon and Hanoi were Taronga's first breeding pair and their first offspring, a female, Elke, was born in early 2009 but, as is common with first-time mothers, Saigon seemed confused by the infant's arrival. Elke had to be hand-raised by Taronga staff who tended to her 24 hours a day for many months, feeding and caring for her in front of Saigon in the hope that it would help her with future newborns.

RIGHT: Saigon and Keo-co.

In 2010, Saigon gave birth to a male infant, Gan Ju ('Orange' in Mandarin) and, this time around, she seemed to understand what the orange coloured thing was, and her mothering instincts kicked in.

A boy, Keo-co (Vietnamese for 'Tug-of-War') was born in 2011, his care shared by mum, Saigon, and another newly arrived female, Meili (Chinese for 'Beautiful'). It was hoped Meili, already an experienced mother, could teach Saigon a thing or two about mothering and keepers noticed Saigon and Meili were quite competitive about who would spend the most amount of time caring for the newborn. Meili was particularly tolerant of Keo-co who liked to jump onto her at great speed and pull at her face and hair.

In 2013, another female, Nuoc ('Water' in Vietnamese), was born to Saigon but this time she could not produce enough milk and keepers took over bottle-feeding in front of the family, giving mother and baby contact with each other through the mesh of the exhibit to ensure the family had a strong connection to the newborn. Nuoc then progressed to play sessions with two male juveniles, Keo-co and Meili's son, Tam Dao (named after a mountain range in Vietnam).

Nuoc was able to rejoin her family months ahead of schedule and, such is the skill of Taronga's primate keepers, that the adult female Leaf-monkeys had been trained to bring the infant over to the mesh of their exhibit so that Nuoc could continue to feed from a bottle the keepers had rigged up.

The Leaf-monkey has been listed as Endangered by the International Union for Conservation of Nature* with just 500 left in Vietnam, and around 1,500 in China. They are scattered between 40 geographically isolated and fragmented populations which, in turn, threatens their genetic viability and therefore survival.

ABOVE: Cheeky Keo-co likes to put everything in his mouth and seemed determined to master solid food early.

LEFT: Remarkably, babies are born with bright orange hair, hardly a camouflage colour, but it's believed to help the females in the group identify them as babies that need to be cared for.

Leaf-monkeys have declined by 50 percent in just three generations, with the major threat coming from hunting and habitat loss, a threat that has been rated as extremely severe in some areas of China where Leaf-monkeys are illegally hunted for the production of 'black ape wine' made specifically from this species.

Two protected areas have been established in Vietnam, and China has 21 protected areas as well as a captive breeding program.

With no other breeding programs in this area initially, Taronga has joined the European Species Management Program to ensure Taronga's genetic diversity becomes part of a larger population.

Francois' Leaf-monkeys are very difficult to observe in the wild because of the nature of their natural terrain, and local observations are complicated by the fact that each area seems to have a different name for the species. Much has been learned from observing these handsome monkeys at Taronga to help breed them successfully and try to safeguard their future.

*Assessed 2008

LEFT: Meili and son, Tam Dao. The females share the care of the infants, cuddling, embracing, social grooming, kissing, carrying and protecting them for up to two years.

Komodo Dragon

Tuka, the impressive Komodo Dragon (*Varanus komodoensis*) at Taronga, is a member of the monitor lizard family. He came to the Zoo as a fully grown, adult male originally having been captured after terrorising villagers on the island of Flores in the Indonesian archipelago. With his rogue behaviour already firmly entrenched, the zookeepers have always had to watch their step around him. Unfortunately, his aggressive behaviour also extended to his own kind which has meant attempts to breed from him have been unsuccessful — with dangerous consequences for his would-be brides and potentially threatening the safety of the keepers who had to come to the females' rescue.

In the wild, survival instinct kicks in immediately the Komodo Dragon egg is hatched. The young Komodo's first action is to climb a nearby tree to avoid being eaten by an adult — or even a parent. (A Komodo cannot chew and instead tears off a chunk of meat, throwing it back into its mouth and swallowing — not a good destiny for any youngster.) Juveniles receive no parental care, remaining up the tree except to feed on insects, small reptiles and birds, until they are big enough to fend off an adult. Fortunately, the weight and size of an adult prevents it from being able to climb.

Komodo Dragons are listed as Vulnerable* by the International Union for Conservation of Nature with fewer than 3,000 remaining in the world, so it is important that zoos like Taronga participate in the international breeding program to ensure the survival of the world's largest lizard.

Komodo Dragons first came to Taronga in 1963 and the Zoo works in partnership with the Komodo Survival Program to jointly protect the Komodo, its local habitat and the food web it relies on to survive.

RIGHT: Tuka, looking every inch the dragon, uses his tongue to detect food, taste the air and, in the wild, can smell his prey up to 8 km away if the carcass is particularly 'aromatic'. Swinging his head from side to side as he walks also helps him test the direction of his prey.

Fossil evidence has shown that the mega-fauna ancestor of the Komodo evolved in Australia before extending into Indonesia where it became isolated as sea levels rose across the continental shelf. Today, most of the world's Komodo population lives in Komodo National Park where its habitat and ecosystems are protected. The park has been listed as a World Heritage site for over 20 years but, over that same period, the Komodo's range and population has decreased so significantly that is likely that the IUCN status of Vulnerable* will be elevated to Endangered.

In 2013, two 16-month-old Komodo Dragons arrived at Taronga and keepers began to train them with coloured target sticks to signal meal times and direct them to opposite ends of their exhibit to feed. In the wild, fights over food are common and, with adults weighing up to 90 kg and stretching up to three metres in length, these disputes are potentially lethal when the Komodos mature.

Komodos are not only apex predators but are among the most actively intelligent of any reptile so it's important for keepers to condition the lizards from a young age to ensure they are raised as good-natured, motivated and mentally stimulated animals. With that sort of up-bringing, the Zoo is optimistic about being able to breed from them successfully in the future when unrelated females will be introduced through the international Komodo match-making program.

*Assessed 1996

TOP: Young Komodo dragon, Naga.

BOTTOM: Young Komodo pair Naga and Bulan bask together under a heat lamp. They do not yet display the aggression of adults who may compete for food.

Sumatran Tiger

Fossil remains show that tigers roamed across Indonesia two million years ago, but the island of Sumatra is now the only place where tigers, rhinos, orang-utans and elephants still live together.

The Sumatran Tiger (*Panthera tigris sumatrae*), found only on Sumatra, is the only surviving member of the Indonesian tigers that included the Bali Tiger and Javan Tiger which became extinct just last century. Sadly, the Sumatran Tiger is heading the same way. As late as 1978, their population was estimated at 1,000. Today, fewer than 400 exist in five national parks and two game reserves, and another 100 in unprotected areas that will soon be lost to agriculture. Over 80 percent of Sumatra's forests have already been felled — largely given over to palm oil and acacia plantations. Human–tiger conflict and illegal trade in body parts also continue to threaten the tigers' existence even though they are protected by law in Indonesia, with tough provisions for jail time and steep fines.

Taronga is part of a collective working to protect Sumatran Tigers. A partnership between zoos around the world and the organisation, 21st Century Tiger, generates funds for tiger conservation through habitat protection and regeneration, and preventing illegal trade. Zoo-based research at Taronga and the provision of infrared equipment for tiger monitoring complement these projects. Taronga, along with other Australian zoos, is running a 'Don't Palm Us Off' campaign against the spread of palm oil plantations.

Taronga also manages the Regional Studbook and Species Management Plan for the species and has successfully bred more than 24 tigers since they were first exhibited at the Zoo in 1916. Their offspring have been distributed over three continents as part of the international breeding program.

RIGHT: When Taronga-born Jumilah was introduced to German-bred Satu, there was an expectation that nature would do the rest. But Satu was so inexperienced, he didn't know he was supposed to mate. A male tiger can kill a female if she is not ready to mate, so zookeepers have to be on high alert. Satu attacked Jumilah on two occasions, forcing keepers to douse him with a high pressure hose. The pair eventually had 180 mating attempts before they became parents.

A group of tigers is called a 'streak', or sometimes an 'ambush' of tigers. Sumatran Tigers are the smallest surviving tiger subspecies and are distinguished by heavy black stripes on their orange coats. The pattern of stripes breaks up their silhouette so they are less visible to their prey. No two tigers have the same stripes and they can be identified by their pattern.

The Sumatran Tiger's smaller size gives it a greater agility for travelling through the thick jungle. Their paws are slightly webbed to help them swim, a major advantage in Sumatra where water is abundant. They will even live in peat swamps, where swimming after prey is often necessary.

At night a tiger can see six times better than a human. They have the largest canine teeth of any land-based carnivore. Their claws are retractable to prevent them from wearing down and to keep them sharp.

In 1916, tigers were among the first animals exhibited at Taronga, with the first Sumatrans exhibited there in 1951, and the first two cubs born in 1980. Jumilah's three cubs, born at Taronga in 2011 represent one percent of the surviving population of Sumatran Tigers worldwide.

The International Union for the Conservation of Nature has listed the Sumatran Tiger as Critically Endangered*, just one step from extinction in the wild.

*Assessed 2008

RIGHT: Mother, Jumilah, was bred at Taronga in 2003 as part of a program to boost dwindling numbers of this Critically Endangered subspecies. Dad Satu gets to see the cubs but, when it comes to raising them, he has to be kept at a safe distance.

Sun Bear

Taronga is used to dealing with rescued animals. Usually they require immediate treatment in the Taronga Wildlife Hospital or are orphaned babies needing around-the-clock hand-rearing by dedicated staff. But rarely had a rescue taken two long and frustrating years to complete after the plight of two Sun Bears (*Helarctos malayanus*) became known to Taronga.

Mr Hobbs and Victoria, were still cubs when they were first saved from a Cambodian restaurant where they were on the menu as Bear Paw Soup. They were days or even hours from being dismembered. Their initial rescuer, an Australian businessman, gave the bears into the care of the Free the Bears organisation which contacted Taronga. Then began the long negotiations with the Cambodian Government to legally bring them to Australia.

The bears' mothers are thought to have been killed trying to protect their cubs when they were forcibly taken from them. The cubs' young lives were then confined to a tiny cage with no room to move around. Victoria and 'Hobbsy', as Mr Hobbs became affectionately known to his keepers, never learnt how to be bears.

Taronga continues to support Free the Bears in a partnership working for the conservation of Asian bears. Free the Bears, in conjunction with the IUCN SSC Bear Specialist Group, Animals Asia, and local government authorities in Vietnam and Cambodia, undertake ranger training, wild habitat surveys and long-term population monitoring to help make the local communities better custodians of the forests and to strengthen the conservation of remaining wild bear populations.

RIGHT: The Sun Bear is named for the bib-shaped golden or white patch on its chest, which local folklore claims represents the rising or setting sun. Each bear's crest is as individual as a fingerprint.

The Sun Bear is the smallest of the world's eight bear species and its stocky, muscular build, small ears and short muzzle has led to it also being known as the 'dog bear'. Its sleek, black coat is thick and coarse to provide protection from twigs, branches and rain but short enough to avoid overheating in the tropical weather.

In spite of their name, Sun Bears are nocturnal. They travel through the forests by night, feeding on termites, ants, beetle larvae, bee larvae and honey, and a large variety of fruits, especially figs when they are in season, as well as shoots of certain palms and flowers.

Mr Hobbs' tragic start to life left him with psychological damage that Taronga's zookeepers and animal behaviourists work on daily to give this special bear the best life possible. His early times at Taronga demonstrated his inability to climb or even to problem solve. He would get into areas in his exhibit but not know how to climb out, and did not know how to look for food — skills Sun Bears normally learn from their mothers during their first two years.

After his companion, Victoria, passed away, at the age of 16 years — thought to be from a weakness caused by her early trauma — Taronga was able to introduce Mr Hobbs to Mary, a boisterous three year old, born at the National Zoo and Aquarium in Canberra. Her mother had also been rescued in Cambodia, and Mary was named after the founder of Free the Bears. Mary had all the education from her mother that Hobbsy missed out on, and their pairing was done at the time when Mary would have naturally left her mother in the wild.

She is confident, playful and mischievous, always active and renowned for rearranging her exhibit, just the way she likes it. She can usually be seen climbing, digging, ripping logs apart, chasing and wrestling with Mr Hobbs or, afterwards, taking bear-naps in her hammock.

LEFT: Sun Bears' jaws provide a powerful bite force, which they use in combination with their long 10 cm claws to tear into the bark of trees to get at the burrowing insects. Their sense of smell is thought to be several thousand times better than that of humans.

Keeping up with Mary has brought a new lease on life to Mr Hobbs. He is becoming more adventurous and she has taught him typical Sun Bear skills. He has even been seen making a valiant attempt to climb a tree and is gradually working harder at looking for food items the zookeepers hide in order to challenge the bears physically and mentally each day. They might include foods wrapped in sacks, buried, or placed in areas the bears need to climb up to. In the wild, Sun Bears spend large amounts of time and energy looking for their food.

The large-scale deforestation throughout Southeast Asia over the past three decades has dramatically reduced suitable habitat and food sources for Sun Bears. The global population has declined by more than 30 percent in three generations and the bears are now extinct in some areas of their former range. They are found sporadically in mainland Southeast Asia as far west as Bangladesh and north-eastern India, as far north as southern Yunnan Province in China, and south and east to Sumatra and Borneo. Sun Bears have been listed as Vulnerable by the International Union of Conservation of Nature*.

At Taronga, when Mary matures, it is hoped that the bear hugs she loves with Mr Hobbs are a good sign they will produce a new genetic line of offspring for the Australian population of Sun Bears.

*Assessed 2008

ABOVE: Mr Hobbs is recognised by his speckled 'bow-tie' shaped sun crest. Mary has a u-shaped necklace mark on her chest.

LEFT: Mr Hobbs shows off his extraordinarily long tongue, ideal for winkling out termites and extracting honey from beehives, giving Sun Bears their other nickname of 'honey bear'.

AUSTRALASIA

Australian Pelican

Taronga Zoo's Great Southern Oceans exhibit is home to two male Australian Pelicans (*Pelecanus conspicillatus*), Mani and Eora. A third pelican, Darren prefers to live elsewhere in the Zoo with other waterbirds.

In the wild, pelicans are highly mobile, searching out suitable areas of water and adequate supplies of food. Although most commonly associated with coastal regions, they can be found in all parts of the country, often observing the world from a lofty perch on a convenient street lamp post.

Pelicans are not capable of sustained flapping flight, but are excellent soarers and can use thermals to rise to considerable altitudes, covering hundreds of kilometres, remaining in the air for up to 24 hours and reaching speeds of up to 56 kilometres per hour. They often fly at an altitude of 1,000 metres, and up to 3,000 metres has been recorded.

Taronga Wildlife Hospital has dealt with as many as 32 pelicans in six weeks after an oil spill, but more usually treats pelicans that have swallowed fish hooks or whose wings or feet have become entangled in fishing lines. Those that can be saved and rehabilitated are returned to the wild, bearing a numbered metal band for any future identification.

Their species has the largest bill of any bird in the world. They mainly eat fish, but are opportunistic feeders and eat a variety of aquatic animals including crustaceans, tadpoles and turtles. They will also rob other birds of their prey and are not averse to stealing scraps from fishermen or queuing with seagulls to accept handouts from humans.

RIGHT: Mani takes a morning constitutional through the Zoo with zookeeper, Jose Altuna, and you'll quite often see him having what looks like a chat with Jose.

During their courtship period, the front half of their pouch becomes bright salmon pink, while the skin of the pouch in the throat region turns chrome yellow. Parts of the top and base of the bill change to cobalt blue, with a black diagonal strip from the base to the tip.

The female digs a nest with her bill and feet. It's not much more than a scrape in the ground lined with any scraps of vegetation or feathers within reach. Both parents share incubation with the eggs held on their feet. The first-hatched chick is substantially larger than its siblings. It receives most of the food and may even attack and kill its nest mates in a survival of the fittest.

Australian Pelicans are not listed as threatened but injuries from human interaction are too often seen at Taronga's Wildlife Hospital.

TOP LEFT: The Australian Pelican Darren shares his waterway at the Zoo with Wandering Whistling-Ducks, Dusky Moorhens and chicks, and Pacific Black Ducks who decided to make Taronga their home.

TOP RIGHT: The pelican uses its sensitive bill to locate fish in murky water, and the hooked ending to help grip any slippery food. Fully extended, its flexible bill can hold up to 13 litres of water. When the pelican has caught its prey, it drains the pouch by drawing it towards its chest, then manoeuvring the catch so the fish's head points down the throat. With a jerk of its head, the pelican swallows its meal in one gulp.

BOTTOM: Eora, Mani and Darren are all rescued Australian Pelicans that could not be rehabilitated into the wild. They participate in the Taronga Seal Show to publicise the plight of their species' interaction with humans. Eora likes to check out the audience from the underwater viewing window. Mani is very confident and comfortable on stage.

Australian Sea-lion

Australian Sea-lions (*Neophoca cinerea*) are the rarest pinnipeds in the world. ('Pinniped' is a generalised name for seals and sea-lions).

In the 18th and 19th centuries, they were extensively hunted for their hide and oil, and even though hunting ceased in the 1920s, their numbers have not recovered, with only 10,000 to 12,000 left in the wild. Occasionally, a wayward sea-lion has been spotted as far north as the mid-north coast of New South Wales but breeding colonies are found only in South Australia and Western Australia. Just five rookeries account for 60 percent of annual pup births.

Sea-lions can dive to depths of up to 300 metres (although 100 metres is more common) for squid, octopus, cuttlefish, fish, small sharks and rock lobsters. They can remain underwater for over eight minutes at a time. Their hind flippers move up and down to propel them forward, similar to a dolphin's tail, and they will often 'porpoise' out of the water when fleeing predators, such as a great white shark, or if they are travelling fast at the surface.

Taronga's breeding program contributes important information to help understand the species, and its Australian Marine Mammal Research Centre studies the species to help ensure their future in the wild.

Taronga's Wildlife Hospital also cares for sick and injured Australian Sea-lions that have beached on the coast of New South Wales, and releases them back into their natural habitat after veterinary treatment and rehabilitation.

RIGHT: Australian Sea-lion pup, Nala, built her muscle strength with play in the water and exploring her habitat on tippy-toes.

LEFT: Sea-lions, like Orson, can walk on land using their large flippers, while seals must wriggle on their bellies because of their much smaller, stubbier flippers. Orson, Taronga's venerable male for many years (and grandfather to Nala), was rescued as a young orphan, but as an adult thrived on participating in the serious research work of testing Sea-lions' sense of smell and cognitive abilities.

BELOW: Taronga's Great Southern Ocean exhibit emulates the marine animals' natural habitat as well as providing spectacular viewing for visitors.

The Australian Sea-lion was listed as Vulnerable under Commonwealth environmental protection in 2005 and is also listed as a Threatened Species in South Australia and Western Australia*.

In the wild, sea-lion pups begin life precariously. Not only do they face man-made threats, but the aggressive nature of sea-lion bulls means many pups have been killed by bite wounds inflicted by males protecting their territory. Females have a long pregnancy of up to 14 months and only breed every two years so, coupled with threats from commercial fishing nets, it's not difficult to see why population numbers keep declining.

At Taronga, zookeepers build close relationships with the sea-lions in their care, and when Kira, was pregnant to Mali in 2009, they were able to regularly ultrasound her and keep a close watch on the development of the youngster. Kira, previously something of a tomboy, was well prepared for the life-changing experience of becoming a first-time mother. She spent the last stages of her pregnancy mostly in her pool, probably to alleviate some of the discomfort of her heavily extended body.

Nala became the first Australian Sea-lion pup born at Taronga in seven years and Kira took to mothering like a 'seal to water'. Within minutes she started making the haunting cries that help a pup identify its mother in large breeding colonies.

Nala was quite uncoordinated in the water at first and had a preference for belly flopping into the pool. When she got tired, she took a break by leaning up against her ever-doting mum or splashing around in the shallow end.

Australian Sea-lions can live up to 20 years of age and Nala has now grown into a silver-grey to fawn colour, like all females of her species. Males are easily distinguished by their much larger bodies and dark brown coats. They get their 'lion' name from the mane-like yellow areas on the neck and top of their heads. Nala is destined to continue to help build on the knowledge base for her kind, and to play her part in carrying her species safely into the future.

*South Australia in 1972; Western Australia in 1950.
Also assessed as Endangered in 2008 by the International Union for Conservation of Nature.

Brolga

There is perhaps no more gracious Australian bird than the pale grey, stilt-legged Brolga (*Grus rubicunda*), best known for its ritualised, elaborate courtship dances.

During mating rituals, Brolgas engage in an extended series of coordinated calls and dance steps. The males usually initiate the display, making loud trumpeting calls. Now and then one bird will pause, throw its head back to trumpet more exuberantly, much like a soloist in an orchestra.

Sometimes just one Brolga dances. Sometimes they dance in pairs, and sometimes a flock of about a dozen dance together, lining up roughly opposite each other, standing with heads thrown back and beaks skyward. The male lifts his wings over his back during the unison calls; the female keeps her wings demurely folded by her sides.

The Brolgas step forward on their stilt legs, their wings half-open, bowing and bobbing their heads, strutting, calling, and sometimes beating their wings as they advance and retreat. From time to time they leap a metre high into the air then parachute back to the ground on outstretched wings.

Taronga's Brolgas generally come to the Zoo as orphaned or injured birds, and the Zoo is committed to their breeding, and educating visitors on the importance of the birds and their habitats.

Bluey is an orphaned Brolga, hand-raised at Taronga after she was found at Evans Head in northern New South Wales in 1972. The Brolgas have their flight feathers clipped

RIGHT: In the wild, the Brolga's long legs keep its body high and dry when wading. It uses its beak to dig and turn over the earth in search of insects, molluscs, crustaceans, frogs or tubers.

to prevent them from flying too far but, one morning, Bluey took fright at a workman's jackhammer and, with an ungainly flapping of her wings, she was able to muster enough feather power to head west towards the Sydney Harbour Bridge. She wasn't used to flying distances and her keeper was confident her muscle strength meant she wouldn't go far. Some long hours later, a local resident on Whiting Beach just west of the Zoo came upon a 'large, grey, friendly flamingo'. When the zookeeper arrived in his little zoo wagon, there was the Brolga. When Bluey saw him, she ran the full length of the beach as fast as her long spindly legs could carry her, with wings outstretched. When she reached him she wrapped her wings around his body, quivering with joy at the sight of him.

In 1981, Bluey eventually joined in elegant dance rituals with Brolga, Padd, and later produced a Brolga chick.

Brolgas are widespread and are often abundant in north and north-east Australia, especially north-east Queensland. Although not considered endangered over the majority of their range, they are sensitive to habitat changes, such as the loss of breeding grounds in shallow marshes, and altered flows in waterways. As a result, populations are showing some decline, especially in southern Australia.

In Victoria the Brolga is listed as Threatened*, and in South Australia and New South Wales it has officially been declared as Vulnerable**.

*Victorian Flora and Fauna Guarantee Act (1988)
** NSW Threatened Species Conservation Act 1995

TOP LEFT: Another Taronga Brolga, Billy stands 1.3 metres tall, but her 2-metre wingspan is even more impressive than her height.

TOP RIGHT: In saltwater marshes, the Brolga can drink salt water and is the only crane species to have a gland in the corner of its eyes to help excrete excessive salt from its body.

BOTTOM: Billy enjoys her walkabouts around the Zoo, designed to stimulate and exercise her. They also serve as a familiarisation measure in case she over-shoots the landing during the Zoo's Free Flight Bird Show and needs to make an 'emergency' landing away from familiar territory.

Goodfellow's Tree Kangaroo

The Goodfellow's Tree-kangaroo, sometimes known as the Ornate Tree-kangaroo (*Dendrolagus goodfellowi*), is said to be descended from pademelons and the very agile rock wallabies. They have evolved quite spectacularly to adapt to an arboreal lifestyle, and are bold and agile in the trees. They climb by wrapping their forelimbs around a trunk or branch and hop with powerful hind legs — limbs that are much less developed than their ground-dwelling cousins — then letting their forelimbs slide forward. Unlike their grounded ancestors, they can move their hind legs independently and even walk backwards — a handy skill when negotiating awkward branches. Treacherously curved front claws and rubbery 'pimpled' pads give them excellent climbing grip.

Unlike a monkey, their remarkably long tail is not prehensile, and is usually held rigidly straight beneath them to serve a similar role to a high-wire walker's balancing pole. When tree-kangaroos are in a hurry, the tail gyrates wildly, constantly rebalancing.

Native to Papua New Guinea, Goodfellow's Tree-kangaroo numbers have declined at least 50 percent over three generations as a result of habitat loss and encroaching human activity. The International Union for the Conservation of Nature has listed them as Endangered*, with some alarming reports estimating only 50 individuals left in the wild.

Taronga is a successful participant in the global breeding program of just 46 Goodfellow's Tree-kangaroos in zoos, of which only 13 are male. Each male is placed with at least two females to optimise breeding success and, in 2013, Taronga's Kwikila gave birth to Nupela, Taronga's first Goodfellow's Tree-kangaroo joey in 20 years.

RIGHT: Kwikila with her joey Nupela starting to survey the outside world.

To date, protected habitats in national parks and reserves have helped ensure their survival, and although they have few, if any, large tree-climbing predators or competitors, they are already extinct in significant parts of their range. Sadly, humans are their main enemy.

Kwikila arrived from Belfast Zoo in January 2013 and her successful pairing with Taronga's resident male, Parum, was a first step in saving this species, one joey at a time.

*Assessed 2008

TOP LEFT: Salsa with her favourite hibiscus snack.

TOP RIGHT: Kwikila and Nupela's colouring helps camouflage them among the decaying vines and mosses at the tops of trees. Their fur, unusually, grows in whorls, supposedly to help rain-shedding. Tree-kangaroos have been known to jump to the ground from heights of 9 metres without injury. Once on the ground, they are quite slow and clumsy, hopping awkwardly, almost at a walking pace, leaning their body far forward to balance their long heavy tail which is often carried arched up and forward in the shape of a question mark.

BOTTOM: Parum courting Salsa. Each tree-kangaroo has a characteristic pair of golden stripes down the centre of its back and a unique pattern of yellow rings and blotches or stripes on its tail.

Greater Bilby

Bilbies are sometimes called rabbit-eared bandicoots and it's because of their 'rabbit ears' that they've become popularised as 'Australia's Easter Bunny' in an attempt by conservationists to raise awareness for the Greater Bilby's precarious plight. How appropriate that 'Australia's Easter Bunny' is a pouched marsupial with young called 'joeys' — like those of kangaroos, koalas and wombats.

The Greater Bilby's cousin, the Lesser Bilby, has not been officially sighted since 1931, although a skull was found in a Wedge-tailed Eagle's nest in 1967 south-east of Alice Springs, and Aboriginal oral history also suggests the species survived until around that time. It's now listed as Extinct by the International Union for Conservation of Nature*.

The Greater Bilby (*Macrotis lagotis*) once roamed across 70 percent of mainland Australia but their population has been in a catastrophic decline since foxes were introduced to the country. It's now found only in north-western Australia where foxes are low in numbers or absent. Predation by cats, and competition from rabbits and livestock, have further driven it to the brink of extinction.

Zoo-based breeding programs, such as the one at Taronga, are needed to maintain the current levels of genetic diversity within the declining population. A Taronga field project in Queensland, developed in conjunction with the Save the Bilby Fund, focuses on a scientific population and habitat viability analysis to guide their recovery.

A second partnership, with the Australian Wildlife Conservancy, monitors wildlife and manages the Scotia Sanctuary, a fox and cat-free nature reserve in the Murray–Darling basin where the Greater Bilby has been re-introduced.

RIGHT: The bilby's long ears can pick up the sound of an insect on the move, and its long hairless snout sniffs out seeds and bulbs that it licks up with a long sticky tongue.

Like the koala, the bilby does not need to drink and gets its moisture from food, which means it's well adapted to Australia's semi-arid and arid outback terrain.

It has poor eyesight and is very much nocturnal, only emerging from its spiralled burrow an hour after sunset and going back underground an hour before dawn. Its long ears help compensate for shortcomings in the eyesight department so that when the bilby digs for food, the tops of its ears can remain above the ground, attuned to the approach of any predators.

The Greater Bilby is already extinct in the wild in New South Wales and, as recently as in the past few decades, has become extinct in parts of Queensland. It is recognised as Critically Endangered* in the rest of the state — one small step from extinction. Conservation programs, such as those at Taronga, are aimed at preventing the most recently discovered species of Bilby — the long-eared Greater Chocolate Bilby (seen outside its burrow only at Easter time) — from becoming the last of the surviving Bilby species.

* Assessed 2008

TOP: In 2014 the Duke and Duchess of Cambridge and their son, Prince George, dedicated the Greater Bilbies exhibit at Taronga Zoo. The bilby which greeted the young prince has been nicknamed George and has been getting a royal share of attention from Zoo visitors since.

BOTTOM: As well as seeds, the bilby's diet includes spiders, worms, insects, bulbs, fruit, fungi and small lizards.

Koala

The Koala (*Phascolarctos cinereus*) is recognised worldwide as a symbol of Australia. Koalas are nocturnal and spend 18 to 20 hours a day sleeping in the fork of a tree. Perhaps it's just as well that a much lesser-known fact is that they are one of the few animals to have evolved a smaller brain to help them conserve energy and survive on their low energy diet!

The Koala's Latin name means 'ash-coloured pouched bear' even though they are not a Koala 'bear' but a marsupial, giving birth to one or sometimes two tiny, blind and hairless young which crawl into the mother's rear-opening pouch where they each attach to one of her two teats for the next six to seven months.

Koalas are often sparsely distributed and difficult to spot in the trees. They range from North Queensland, through NSW and Victoria down the east coast of Australia and around to South Australia. After being heavily hunted for fur in the early 20th century, they were also introduced to a dozen islands off the mainland in an effort to save them from extinction.

Taronga's vets are undertaking a long-term research project into Koala health, studying their immune systems to understand the impact of common Koala viruses. Results of these studies are made available to wildlife care professionals.

Just about anywhere where there are 100 of the right type of eucalypt trees, there is a potential Koala habitat (they need that many trees per koala to exist in the wild). Koalas eat up to 1 kg of leaves a day and, with a diet exclusively of eucalyptus, their bodies even take on a eucalyptus odour.

RIGHT: As Koala joeys build up their strength and confidence they will begin to venture away from mum to play and to snuggle with other young joeys.

Around Sydney, river red gums, grey gums and mahogany eucalypts are their trees of choice. In northern NSW, you may spot a Koala in tallowwood and forest red gum. Manna gums head their wish list in the south, and in the west Koalas seem to prefer river red gum and ribbon gum.

In 2014, Taronga, in partnership with Greening Australia planted over 9,000 of the Koalas' preferred eucalypts at the University of Western Sydney to ensure the Zoo's Koala population has the correct diversity of leaves for their diet. To guard against the possibility of bushfires, drought or insect attacks, Taronga has four eucalyptus plantations to guarantee a steady supply of Koala food.

The Koala's enormous black, leathery, spoon-shaped nose helps it differentiate between eucalyptus varieties it likes and those it ignores. They favour the young and juicy eucalyptus leaves that are both high in oils and high in toxins which are avoided by most mammals (except Ringtail Possums and Greater Gliders) but the Koala's gut has a long thin appendix to break down the poison.

They seldom drink but have been known to approach humans for a drink of water during extreme droughts.

TOP LEFT: Juvenile Koalas enjoy cuddling up together, like 18-month-old joeys, Sydney and Milli, snuggled up with 12-month-old Tucker. If little Tucker fell asleep first, the girls often used him as a comfy pillow, one on top of the other.

TOP RIGHT: Little joey, Lincoln, takes a glimpse at the outside world from the safety of mum's pouch. He was born tiny and hairless six months earlier, then clung to a teat inside the pouch. He will emerge when he is strong enough to hang onto mum's belly or back, even while he sleeps.

BOTTOM: A Koala family unit. In the wild, when joeys are between one and three years old, they leave their mother's home range to live independent lives.

LEFT: Even mum's furry head can be a comfortable snooze spot in the shade.

BELOW: Joey, Bai'yali, shows a liking for young eucalyptus shoots. She has a built-in resistance to the leaves' toxins and can start testing her new food as soon as she emerges from mum's pouch.

They have two thumbs and three fingers on each front paw to help them grip evenly on each side of a branch. Two of their hind toes have also fused together to form a handy two-pronged comb for grooming as well as for removing ticks.

Surprisingly, like humans and the higher primates, Koalas have individual fingerprints. Unlike us, however, they have 11 pairs of ribs instead of 13, and feel uneasy if picked up under their arms. They also have a curved spine that makes it more comfortable for them to sit on branches and in tree forks for long periods of time.

In the breeding season, Taronga's males Max and Darwin can be heard advertising themselves with loud growling coughs and bellows. Their bellows sound quite incongruous out of the mouths of these cuddly, furry creatures; like a deep snore followed by a belch. The bellows vary according to body size to let the females know how big and attractive the male is, and to intimidate rivals. Koala mating songs range from pig-like grunts and growls made by the males, to high pitched trembling sounds by the females.

There is only one species of Koala and any differences in fur and body size are said to be the result of environmental conditions. Northern Koalas tend to have shorter, silver-grey fur, and those in the south are nearly twice the size and have longer, thicker, brown-grey fur.

Where trees are scarce or habitat has been reduced to isolated pockets, Koalas are forced to travel along the ground more often where they are more vulnerable to dog attacks. And if they live in high concentrations as a result of deforestation or bushfires, the widespread presence of chlamydia, a bacterial disease, also becomes a problem.

The Koala is listed as Vulnerable* but, sadly, continuing loss of their habitat may see this famous Australian elevated to Endangered.

*Koalas in Queensland, NSW and ACT are considered most at risk, assessed by the Australian Government under national environment law, 2012

Little Penguin

The Little Penguin (*Eudyptula minor novaehollandiae*), also known as the Blue Penguin is, surprisingly, the sole penguin that calls Australia home, even though all species of penguins are native to the southern hemisphere. Home for the Little Penguin is along the southern edge of mainland Australia as far north as Port Macquarie, down to Tasmania and across to New Zealand and the Chatham Islands.

The Little Penguin can draw itself up to a height of 40 to 45 cm and hops onto the scales at around 1 kg, making it the smallest of the world's 17 species of penguins.

They can form long-term pairs but if breeding success is low, that's grounds for divorce, and researchers have recorded new partnerships at an annual rate of between 18 and 50 percent in nesting colonies.

At Taronga, long-time pair, Brooke and Drill, had been a faithful and successful breeding pair for seven years until they were split by the devious antics of a one-legged, rescued penguin, Billy. Don't be fooled by Little Penguins' diminutive size and innocent looks, for Billy strategically befriended several of the male birds to eventually form a gang. He then led them on a savage attack on Brooke, injuring his opponent's right eye so badly that Brooke had to be hospitalised. This was Billy's chance. He quickly ingratiated himself with Drill who was too soon led astray. On Brooke's return, it was all over bar the shouting, or in this case, the 'kak kak kaks' and some more intimidating displays of aggression from Billy and his mates.

With Manly almost on Taronga's doorstep, the Zoo closely monitors the Little Penguin colony there and its immediate habitat, providing nesting boxes and undertaking all-important educational campaigns to schools, local residents, tourists and Zoo visitors. The Manly colony has now grown to 65 Little Penguins and the local community takes an active role in protecting it.

10,000 slate-blue downy feathers provide insulation in the cool waters — up to four times the feather density of flighted birds. The Little Penguin eats around a third of its body weight each day and will dive from six to 69 metres to catch fish, including anchovies, pilchards, whitebait and squid, remaining under water for over a minute at a time.

Although relatively common in the southern waters of Australia, most breeding pairs ashore live in colonies on the safety of islands. All mainland New South Wales colonies have become extinct except for the protected colony at Manly on the shores of Sydney Harbour — listed as Endangered in 1997 when only an estimated 35 birds remained.

During the moulting season Little Penguins shed their old feathers and grow new ones over a period of around 15 days. During this time they are not waterproof and so stay ashore where, unfortunately, they are vulnerable to dog, cat and fox attacks.

Taronga Wildlife Hospital plays a vital role in the rehabilitation and release of injured Little Penguins, treating up to 40 each year for injuries related to moulting, animal attacks, and boating propeller injuries. Most are returned to sea after rehabilitation.

TOP: A Little Penguin, ready for release back into the wild, checks the coast is clear before leaving the safety of his travel box.

BOTTOM: This trio of penguins was found on Sydney's eastern suburbs beaches with flipper injuries, and were thin, weak, dehydrated and vulnerable to attack from predators after coming ashore for their annual moult. Surf lifesavers and local residents came to the rescue to deliver the birds into Taronga's Wildlife Hospital where they were given a thorough veterinary examination including x-rays and blood tests before eventually being returned to the sea after their new waterproof feathers had grown.

Fiordland Crested Penguin

A close neighbour of the Little Penguins at Taronga is Mr Munro, the bushy-eyebrowed Fiordland Crested Penguin (*Eudyptes pachyrhynchus*) from the sub-Antarctic seas of New Zealand. Mr Munro, like the others of his species, is listed as Vulnerable* by the International Union for Conservation of Nature.

He was found 2,000 kilometres from home after a fishing trip that went slightly off course. He washed up near Nora Head on the New South Wales Central Coast in 2006 after a heroic swim across the Tasman Sea. He'd been in the water so long he'd grown barnacles on his tail feathers and was weak and drastically underweight. He was brought to Taronga Zoo's Wildlife Hospital to be nursed back to health.

Taronga is the only zoo in the world caring for Fiordland Crested Penguins, all of whom were washed up on Australian beaches at different times over a number of years. Because of the danger of introducing disease to this most endangered penguin species in the world — even after lengthy quarantine — none of the Fiordland Crested Penguins can be returned to their natural habitat.

High hopes were held that Mr Munro would breed with Taronga's two females, Chalkie and Milford, to add to the 1,000 breeding pairs that remain in the wild. Sadly, the best laid plans of conservationists were subject to Mr Munro's whims. He decided the females were not to his taste as mates, and the patter of little Fiordland Crested Penguin feet has not been heard around the Zoo.

Perhaps, one day, another female marathon swimmer may be more to his liking but until that time Mr Munro delights in tormenting his Little Penguin neighbours who take it all in their little stride.

*Assessed 2001

Mr Munro stalks past his Little Penguin neighbours with the weight of the future of his species on his shoulders.

New Zealand Fur-seal

It can be confusing trying to tell the difference between a seal and a sea-lion, especially the New Zealand Fur-seal also known as the Kekeno, or the Antipodean Fur-seal (*Arctocephalus forsteri*) which, like a sea-lion — and unlike a true seal — has external ear flaps, and hind flippers that it can rotate forward for faster movement on land. It differs from sea-lions in its smaller size and pointy nose.

Fur-seals were hunted for their pelt until the late 19th century, by which time their population had plummeted by 90 percent, pushing them to the brink of extinction. Fortunately they are now officially protected in both New Zealand waters and around Australia, and their numbers have recovered to around 200,000 individuals — half are found in New Zealand waters, half in Australian.

The Australian Marine Mammal Research Centre, located in Taronga's Great Southern Oceans precinct, observes foraging behaviours and interaction by the seals, providing a unique understanding of their wild counterparts. Taronga and its research partners track fur-seals fitted with GPS and time-depth-recorders to gather information on haul-out behaviour, habitat preferences, and the population structure beyond New South Wales. This has important implications for conserving the fur-seal population as a whole, rather than just protecting the animals resident in a protected marine park.

Taronga Wildlife Hospital has seen a number of injured New Zealand Fur-seals in recent years, often the result of shark attacks as well as attacks by aggressive male sea-lions. Where possible, the seals will be returned to the wild after treatment and recuperation, but if their age or the extent of care required for their recovery makes this impossible, their permanent home becomes Taronga's Great Southern Oceans exhibit.

The family of eared seals includes sea-lions and fur-seals. They used their front flippers for swimming whereas 'true seals' use their hind flippers.

TOP LEFT: Young Bondi, after being admitted to the Taronga Wildlife Hospital, showing the lesser of some of his injuries from a shark attack off Bondi Beach.

TOP RIGHT: Bondi ready for breakfast, showing his healed shark bite.

ABOVE: Bondi is spending a few years growing up and splashing about with the other young seals at Taronga before training for the Seal Show. He's the smallest of Taronga's seals, but has the biggest attitude and determination for survival.

In 2013, Bondi (named after the beach where he was rescued) was brought to the Taronga Wildlife Hospital with wounds covering nearly two thirds of his young body. He survived against the odds, spending several weeks in the Wildlife Intensive Care Unit, receiving treatment for his wounds and recovering from malnourishment with a hospital diet of tasty pilchards. Sadly, the extent of his injuries and long rehabilitation meant he couldn't be returned to the wild.

Like Ronnie, who also survived a shark attack in 2008, and now calls Taronga home, Bondi will eventually take his place in the Taronga Seal Show. What seals are trained to do may look like tricks, but Ronnie has been taught skills that could save his life. At first he was trained for 'husbandry behaviours' designed to let keepers check his health, examine his teeth, inspect his flippers and even lift his eyelids in search of an injury. Without the animal's willingness to cooperate, if keepers suspected a tooth injury or a fish bone stuck in his lip, vets would have to anaesthetise the animal to attend to it. Now, keepers can just lift Ronnie's lip to check on him, something that can take a few minutes instead of a whole day in hospital.

Seals are highly inquisitive and part of their training puts them through mock medical procedures to get them used to instruments and equipment, using tourniquets and x-ray tables, and being around vets wearing lead radiology gowns. That means, when it comes to the real thing, the seals are more relaxed about cooperating — especially knowing there is a tasty seafood reward for good behaviour at the end.

Nearly every animal at Taronga is trained to receive inspections for health care. And Taronga's tigers and Komodo Dragons have been among the most cooperative!

For Ronnie and Bondi, only when these husbandry behaviours have been established can training begin for behaviours used specifically for the Seal Show. Six years after arriving at the zoo as an injured pup, Ronnie is able to present the entire Seal Show and enjoys continuing his learning every day.

Platypus

A rubbery, duck-like bill, dark brown fur, webbed front feet and shy nature have made the Platypus one of Australia's most unusual and intriguing animals. Perhaps that's also a reason why it's been too difficult to officially agree on a collective noun for a group of Platypuses (and because they tend to be solitary).

The Platypus or Duck-billed Platypus (*Ornithorhynchus anatinus*) and the Echidna are the world's only egg-laying mammals, called 'monotremes'. Monotremes lay eggs like birds, have no teats, and raise their young like mammals.

They may look enticingly cuddly, but the males have a pair of venomous spurs on their hind legs and, although the venom won't kill a human, the pain they inflict is excruciating.

For 20 years, attempts at breeding Platypuses at Taronga had been unsuccessful and, although they are not listed as Endangered, if zoos are unable to breed Platypuses in captivity there is no recovery safeguard if the species became threatened in the wild.

Knowledge of the behaviour of these elusive animals comes mainly from observing them in zoos. Without being able to successfully breed them, their basic life statistics — such as how long they suckle their young and how much they like to eat — remain unknown. So when Taronga's female Platypus Maryanne and male, Abi, became the proud parents of two babies — it was regarded as an important breakthrough.

Taronga is also working with the Australian Platypus Conservancy and the University of New South Wales to raise awareness of the use of 'opera house' style yabby traps — deadly to Platypuses — as well as researching alternative, humane, yabby trapping methods.

RIGHT: The Platypus is smaller than many people imagine, with the males only about 50 cm long and weighing just 1.5 kg. The females are slightly smaller.

The Platypus appears to have been first displayed to the Australian public in 1910 at the Sydney Zoological Garden, the forerunner to Taronga, then located at Moore Park. One animal was successfully maintained in a system of tanks and tunnels, eating a mixed diet of freshwater shrimps, earthworms, beetle grubs and pond snails but had to be released into another urban pond when the approaching winter created difficulties in providing an adequate food supply. Even today, the cost of purchasing substantial quantities of crayfish, along with the large amount of staff time devoted to keeping tanks and surroundings meticulously clean, mean that the Platypus is one of the most expensive native mammals to keep in zoos.

Platypuses have no teeth, and store food in cheek pouches, bringing their food to the water surface before grinding it between their jaws' horny plates and ridges. When not foraging, they spend most of the time in their burrows.

In winter, the male initiates courtship with aquatic displays such as rolling sideways with the female platypus — diving, touching, passing, and grasping the female's tail in his bill.

The pregnant female will block herself into the burrow with dirt to keep the nesting chamber at an even temperature and humidity, and to protect her young from flooding and predators. After laying two sticky, soft-shelled eggs, she incubates the eggs by holding them to her belly with her tail. Although the tiny young are born naked, blind and with undeveloped limbs, they can suckle on mammary patches where milk oozes onto the mother's skin.

The International Union for Conservation of Nature* lists the status of the Platypus as not threatened, as do the Australian Government and relevant State Governments. Nonetheless, there is evidence that Platypus populations have declined precipitously in many parts of their range, and now appear to be extinct in South Australia.

The Platypus's low population density, low reproductive rates, and the high female mortality rates when they are forced to compete for food with larger and more aggressive males, mean we cannot be complacent about the survival of this iconic and unique Australian.

*Assessed 2001

LEFT: Awkward out of the water, the Platypus waddles with the webs of its front feet turned back so it can use its claws for digging.

BELOW: The Platypus lives in freshwater rivers, creeks and ponds along eastern Australia from Queensland to Tasmania. When the water is cold, the Platypus is cleverly able to increase its body heat up to around 32°C.

Regent Honeyeater

The spectacular Regent Honeyeater (*Anthochaera phrygia*), one of Australia's most handsome honeyeaters, was once celebrated as the Embroidered Honeyeater, the Flying Coachman and the Warty-faced Honeyeater, after the large patch of bare, bumpy skin around its eyes. Its namers unkindly forgot its dominant feature, the beautiful black and yellow lace scalloping on its body.

It was once found across four states from Rockhampton in Queensland to the Mount Lofty Ranges in South Australia but, with the loss of its habitat, it is now restricted to small patches inland of the Great Dividing Range in New South Wales and Victoria. It once congregated in flocks of 50 to 100, but today is found singly or in small groups of up to ten. Population estimates range from 500 to 1,500, causing it to be listed as Endangered by four State and Territory Governments and Critically Endangered in New South Wales. Its decline has had a significant impact on native plant species that depend on it as an important pollinator.

A national recovery plan involving Taronga and other wildlife organisations has been established to save this species from extinction. Taronga has been breeding Regent Honeyeaters since 1995 and, in 2008, 27 birds were released at Mt Pilot National Park in Victoria and have successfully bred. In early 2010, 44 more were released to help rebuild wild populations , and in 2014 a further 77 were released. A variety of over 10,000 trees have also been planted to provide a critical habitat with blossoms year-round. The recovery plan also includes the protection of their habitat from clearing, logging and firewood collection, as well as planting the eucalypts they feed on.

RIGHT: Males are identified by the yellow, warty bare skin surrounding dark eyes. The females are smaller, have less black on their throat and have a bare, yellow patch only below their eyes. Immature birds have browner feathers and a paler bill.

Southern Corroboree Frog

The dramatic decline of some frog species has had experts describing the loss of frogs globally as the largest mass extinction since the dinosaurs.

Australia's striking, black-and-yellow Corroboree Frogs are among the most visually spectacular frogs in the world but they are perilously close to extinction in the wild. They live only within Kosciuszko National Park where they depend on the extremes of snow, ice, spring flooding as well as summer sunshine to trigger the various stages of their lifecycle.

The Southern Corroboree Frog (*Pseudophryne corroboree*) has suffered a catastrophic population decline since the mid-1980s and, in January 2014, as few as six males were found at nesting sites with no evidence of a next generation. They have been listed by international, national and state bodies as Critically Endangered.

The frogs' colouring shows other animals and birds that they are toxic and their rapid decline is mainly the result of a disease caused through an amphibian fungus, known as Chytrid.

They are also particularly susceptible to climate change and, in seasons with a reduced snow and ice cover, ironically, tadpoles may be over-exposed to sub-zero temperatures. Then, with a smaller snow melt, nest sites may not flood sufficiently for the hatched tadpoles to reach nearby pools where they can metamorphose into adult frogs in summer. Warm summers, too, lead to more prolific weed growth which casts too much shade over pools, preventing successful breeding conditions. Feral pigs, feral horses, and Samba deer, which trample the frogs' wetland habitat, also reduce the suitability of breeding areas.

It's no wonder that frogs generally are regarded as a barometer of the health of our environment, the outdoor equivalent of the singing canary in the mineshafts.

Southern Corroboree Frogs in a living sphagnum nest at Taronga.

LEFT: The adult Southern Corroboree Frog is only 2.5 to 3 cm long.

BELOW: Taronga herpetologists work with expert rangers from the NSW National Parks and Wildlife Service to release hatchings back into a remote area of Kosciuszko National Park.

Adult males move into breeding areas in early to late summer, and call to attract the females. If a female is attracted, she will lay her eggs in his nest and then move on. The male remains in his nest through the breeding season, trying to attract more females and to accumulate many clutches.

After hatching, the tadpoles use groundwater to wriggle out of the nest sites and into nearby pools where they live until they metamorphose into frogs in early summer.

Breeding programs in safe zoo-based environments are essential for the long-term survival of this species, and Taronga's breeding program released over 2,000 Southern Corroboree Frog eggs between 2011 and 2014 back into Kosciuszko National Park in fungus-free areas. Taronga also retains a viable breeding and 'insurance' population at the Zoo's custom-built facilities for releases in future years.

If you think breeding frogs is as easy as catching some tadpoles in a jar of creek water, and watching over them until they turn into frogs, think again.

Herpetologists had a lot to learn about being able to successfully breed this Critically Endangered sub-alpine amphibian. Climate-controlled facilities are needed to replicate seasonal changes, with light-sensitive switches to stimulate alpine light conditions. Water has to be carbon-filtered and reconstituted with trace elements to suit the frogs' sensitive skin. When handling any equipment or animals, scientists observe high levels of biosecurity, wearing dedicated footwear, protective lab coats and powder-free gloves. The frogs' food is enriched with a dusting of calcium and multivitamins. Live sphagnum moss is grown in gravel for nesting, and the adult frogs need to be rotated between breeding groups and single-sex groups according to the season. Tadpoles are reared in aquariums. There is even ambient music, with tape-recorded male frog calls played to encourage competition among males to call to the females in the breeding season.

Many frogs eat insect pests and, in their turn, are food for other animals, so re-establishing frogs in their natural habitats is one of the most important hop, step and gigantic leaps we can do to ensure the survival of viable ecosystems.

Southern Hairy-nosed Wombat

Wombats have, unkindly, been called 'muddle-headed', perhaps because of their slow metabolism and pugnacious and persistent attempts to travel in a direct path, no matter what obstacles lie in their way. In fact, they have the largest brain, relative to body size, of any marsupial.

The Southern Hairy-nosed Wombat (*Lasiorhinus latifrons*), a stocky, robust marsupial, is distinguished from the Common Wombat by its silky fur, longer ears and furry muzzle.

Any predator who tries to attack a wombat from behind is in for a surprise. Wombats have a natural armour-plating, a hard dinner plate-like shield of cartilage under the skin at the back of their bodies. And anyone foolish enough to follow a wombat down its burrow risks having its head or body parts crushed against the roof or sides of the burrow.

One of the important roles the Southern Hairy-nosed Wombat plays at Taronga is that it shares behaviours with its cousin, the Critically Endangered Northern Hairy-nosed Wombat, of which there are fewer than 115 left in one protected Queensland national park (with perilously fewer breeding females than males). Through Taronga Zoo's Southern Hairy-nosed Wombat conservation breeding program, and other similar programs, scientists are able to learn more about the social, reproductive and breeding behaviours of the Northern Hairy-nosed Wombat in the hope that its numbers can recover from the brink of extinction.

Although the Southern Hairy-nosed Wombat numbers are still abundant and its risk of extinction is officially classified as of Least Concern*, it is subject to habitat loss as land is used for agriculture. A debilitating parasitic infestation of Sarcoptic Mange that results in a slow and painful death is now also of concern (previously only affecting the Common Wombat).

*Assessed by the International Union for the Conservation of Nature, 2008

Wombats have a cleft upper lip that lets them eat the smallest of grass shoots close to the ground despite their large head, teeth and powerful jaws. They also generally only drink when it rains so they are well developed for survival in their natural habitat. But when it rains they have been known to stand in puddles for up to half an hour, slowly drinking.

Tasmanian Devil

High-pitched screams, spine-chilling guttural growls, fierce snarls, lunging and teeth-baring displays were why the early European settlers in Australia dubbed the Tasmanian Devil (*Sarcophilus harrisii*) a 'devil'.

The Devil utters these diabolic sounds to express its dominance during the mating season as well as at meal times when otherwise solitary Devils may come together to feed on a carcass. Strangely enough, the Devil's famous wide open-mouthed gape that looks so threatening, is more likely to be an expression of fear or uncertainty. And when it challenges another Devil to a fight, this fearsome animal does so with a strong sneeze. If that doesn't work, he bravely increases the threat level to loud snorts and threatening calls.

The Tasmanian Devil stands at just 76 cm, which is enough to make it the largest carnivorous marsupial in the world.

The species disappeared from the Australian mainland around 400 years ago, thought to be from competition with Australia's other main carnivore, the Dingo. In Tasmania, their numbers declined as early Europeans trapped and killed Tasmanian Devils for over 100 years, believing that they would eat their farm animals.

Tasmanian Devils have been protected since 1941, but their population has decreased by more than 60 percent in the past decade, with an even greater rate of decline threatened in the near future. Most of this decline is due to Devil Facial Tumour Disease, a fatal infectious cancer that is most easily spread between Devils through biting — a common behaviour during the mating season. The Tasmanian Devil is now listed as Endangered*.

The highest priority to help avoid total extinction is to establish insurance populations of healthy Devils away from infected populations, such as in mainland zoos.

The Tasmanian Devil's ears flush red to show its aggression. Theo is one of the Tasmanian Devil dads fiercely helping to save its species at Taronga.

Taronga's Tasmanian Devil breeding program is based on carefully selected pairs to maximise genetic diversity in any insurance population. Taronga's Devils and other zoo breeding populations may need to carry the species for 25 to 50 years before they can be reintroduced to their natural habitat, should the Devils (and the disease) become extinct in the wild.

Devils are nocturnal and rely on their keen sense of smell to locate a carcass in the night. Their stocky bodies are not built to run at high speeds to chase down prey so they tend to scavenge carrion, including road kill (sadly, too often ending up as another victim themselves). They like getting their teeth into almost any meat, wholly devouring hair, organs, and bones, and sometimes digging up dead animals to feast on the rotting bodies. They are gorge feeders, capable of eating up to 10 percent of their own bodyweight of food in a day. Like other marsupials, they store extra fat in their tails, so unhealthy animals can be easily recognised by their limp, skinny tails.

The female Devil is 'highly social' in the breeding season, showing little fidelity to her mate and visiting several males in quick succession even though each will physically try to prevent her from leaving in order to protect his paternity.

Dens are typically underground wombat burrows, rock piles, caves and dense vegetation near riverbanks. In settled areas, dens can also be found under buildings — quite disconcerting if it happens to be your house.

*Assessed under the Tasmanian Government's Threatened Species Protection Act in 2008 and the Australian Federal Government in 2009.

TOP LEFT: The mother Devil gives birth to 20 to 30 tiny, pink and hairless, undeveloped babies, called imps or joeys. Using their claws, they clamber from the birth canal to the mother's rear-facing pouch, where they compete to attach themselves to one of only four available teats. They remain in her pouch for close to four months.

TOP RIGHT: The Devil's oversized head, sharp teeth and strong, muscular jaws — strong enough to gnaw through a metal trap — can deliver, pound for pound, one of the most powerful bites of any mammal.

BOTTOM RIGHT: Taronga Zoo's Tasmanian Devil breeding program is a key tool in the fight to save the species from extinction, working with other zoos and wildlife parks across Australia.

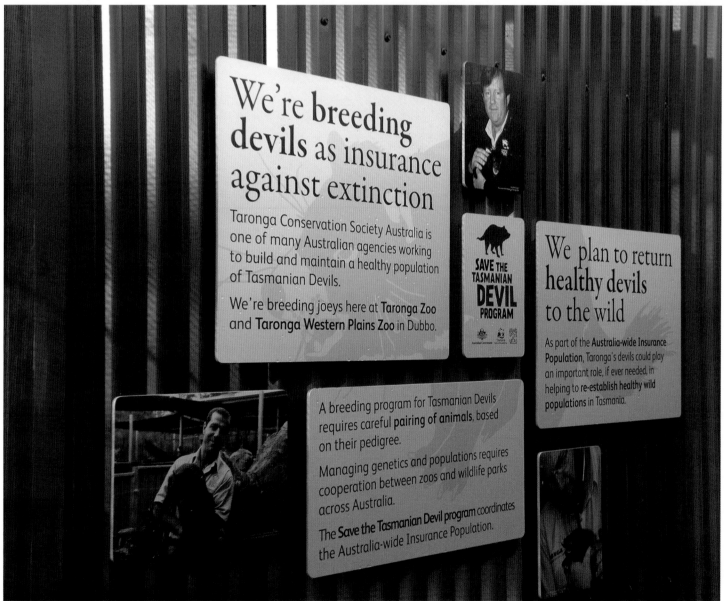

We're breeding devils as insurance against extinction

Taronga Conservation Society Australia is one of many Australian agencies working to build and maintain a healthy population of Tasmanian Devils.

We're breeding joeys here at **Taronga Zoo** and **Taronga Western Plains Zoo** in Dubbo.

SAVE THE TASMANIAN DEVIL PROGRAM

We plan to return healthy devils to the wild

As part of the **Australia-wide Insurance Population**, Taronga's devils could play an important role, if ever needed, in helping to **re-establish healthy wild populations** in Tasmania.

A breeding program for Tasmanian Devils requires careful **pairing of animals**, based on their pedigree.

Managing genetics and populations requires cooperation between zoos and wildlife parks across Australia.

The **Save the Tasmanian Devil program** coordinates the Australia-wide Insurance Population.

Wedge-tailed Eagle

The Wedge-tailed Eagle (*Aquila audax*) is the largest bird of prey in Australia, and one of the largest in the world. It's easily recognised by the diamond or wedge-shaped tail in flight, as well as its heavily-feathered legs, making it look a little as though it's wearing fluffy pantaloons.

The Wedge-tailed Eagle is widespread across Australia, including Tasmania and on offshore islands, such as Flinders Island, Maria Island and Kangaroo Island. It can be found in almost all habitats but predominantly in lightly timbered and open woodland areas.

The Tasmanian subspecies is listed as Endangered*. The mainland species is not endangered but is legally protected by Australian law.

The Wedge-tailed Eagle plays a role in the environment keeping down the numbers of feral animals such as foxes, hare, rabbits and feral cats, as well as cleaning up roadkill. Taronga's Wedge-tailed Eagles have come to the Zoo because of injuries that required treatment in the Taronga Wildlife Hospital or needed to be rehabilitated and restored to health for a variety of reasons. The few who were not suitable to return to the wild have remained at the Zoo.

This powerful bird of prey hunts wallabies, kangaroos, possums, young goats and lambs, as well as lizards, snakes and birds. It's capable of taking prey up to several times its own weight, and sometimes hunts cooperatively in pairs or even in small groups.

During drought conditions, eagles may not breed for many years but in good times, as the breeding season approaches, a mating pair will perch close together and preen each other. They will also perform dramatic aerobatic displays with the male diving towards the female at breakneck speed, pulling out of his dive at the last moment and rising back above her on outstretched wings. She will then either ignore him or fly upside down to perform aerial loop-the-loops together.

* Listed under the Environment Protection and Biodiversity Act 1999.

ABOVE: Her mid-brown colouring signifies that Gina is still a young bird. She will turn dark brown at around ten years of age. Her keen eyesight sees infrared and ultraviolet light, helping her to spot prey and even to see rising thermals on which she can soar.

RIGHT: When emaciated Cersei was found, unable to fly because of abnormal feather development, trainer Erin Stone took the young eagle under her wing. 18 months later, now fully-fledged, it seems, Cersei is returning the favour.

THE
AMERICAS

Andean Condor

The majestic Andean Condor (*Vultur gryphus*) is one of the world's largest and heaviest birds able to fly and, when it takes off, needs all of its considerable strength and 3-metre wingspan to launch its bodyweight off the ground. An adult male stands at 1.5 metres — so tall it could easily look you in the eye should you happen to meet nose to beak.

The high windy altitudes and thermal air currents of South America's Andean Mountains help the Condor conserve energy and glide on the currents to soar hundreds of kilometres for hours at a time in search of food. It ranges as far down as the coastal plains and even lowland deserts, but can also soar so high that, in Incan times, it was thought to be a messenger from the sun god, lifting the sun into the sky each day and returning it to a sacred lake each night.

As one of the vulture family, condors are nature's clean-up squad, feeding on dead and decaying carcasses but, although they can stomach maggot-encrusted meat in advanced stages of decomposition, they are vulnerable to the illegal poisons farmers use to kill Mountain Lions and foxes. This, together with their slow breeding and dwindling food supplies as more land is given over to farming, has led to their being listed as Near-Threatened by the International Union for Conservation of Nature*.

The Andean Condor is in danger of extinction in its natural habitat and its survival may depend on captive breeding programs.

Condors mate for life and in the wild live to around 50 years. They breed only once in two years with the chick dependent on its parents, often until it has to make way for a new sibling.

*Assessed 2001

RIGHT: Konira was the fifth Andean Condor egg to hatch at the Zoo. She has been hand-reared to give her the best chance of survival. And surviving she is, after putting on half of her adult weight in her first three months.

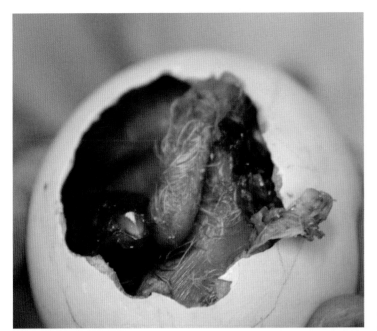

Cotton-top Tamarin

Sometimes called the 'punk primate', the Cotton-top Tamarin (*Saguinus oedipus*) is visually distinctive with its mohawk crest of long white hair from its forehead to nape, flowing into a mane over its shoulders.

Part of the most diminutive family of monkeys, the Cotton-top is highly sociable and communicates using grammatical rules in its vocalisations with unusually sophisticated bird-like whistles, soft chirps, high-pitched trills and staccato calls. When coming into contact with other groups that threaten their territory, the communication of choice, however, is to threateningly show its rear end.

The group's social behaviour extends to cooperative breeding, beginning with the father assisting at the birth by receiving the young and doing more than his fair share of carrying the babies (usually twins). Siblings and older adults also help in rearing the offspring of the dominant pair. The dominant female also uses pheromones to suppress the sexual behaviour of subordinate females in the group and, although unrelated males that join the group can release the females from this reproductive spell, remarkably, only one pregnancy per group will be successful.

At Taronga's Learning Centre, a group of four Cotton-top brothers, Wan, Trichidae, twins JD and Petey, arrived in 2014 to help in the Zoo's educational program to prevent illegal wildlife trade and promote the plight of their Critically Endangered species.

Cotton-top Tamarins are listed as Critically Endangered* by the International Union for the Conservation of Nature, because of an 80 percent reduction in population over the past three generations, a direct result of habitat loss and illegal pet trade. Only 6,000 remain in the wild.

*Assessed 2008

At Taronga's Learning Centre, the Cotton-tops enjoy a tasty diet of maggots, mealworms, locusts and fruit and vegetables, along with an occasional flower as a special treat.

Green Iguana

Although often referred to as the Common Iguana, the Green Iguana (*Iguana iguana*) is far from ordinary. They have a white photo-sensory organ on the top of their heads, sometimes called a third eye (most other lizards have lost this feature) and although the 'eye' has only a rudimentary retina and lens, it is sensitive to light and dark, allowing the Iguana to detect the movement of a predator above.

Green Iguanas are both arboreal and terrestrial, and are agile climbers as well as swimmers. They can drop 15 metres from a rock face or tree and land unhurt.

In the water, the iguana lets its four legs hang limply by its sides, and propels itself through the water with powerful tail strokes. Out of the water, it snorts excess saline out through its two prominent nostrils to regulate its body's salt level.

Green Iguanas have leaf-like shaped, very sharp teeth, with serrated edges that can shred foliage as well as human skin. One of the first dinosaur fossils discovered was named *Iguanodon* because of its similar teeth, and led to the (incorrect) assumption that it had resembled a giant iguana.

Taronga's male iguana, Jub Jub, is the largest of three Green Iguanas at Taronga and came to the Zoo after being rescued by National Parks and Wildlife staff who found him as an illegal pet in 2005. He sired his first offspring in 2012, one male and four females.

Contrary to their name, Green Iguanas come in a spectacular range of colours. In the southern end of their range, in countries such as Peru, they are blue with bold blue markings. On South Caribbean islands, they vary from green to lavender, to black and even pink. In the western region of Costa Rica they are red in colour and, in the north of their range, in countries such as Mexico, they come in orange tones.

A row of spines along their backs and tails help protect iguanas from predators. They use their tails to painfully strike an opponent and, like many other lizards, the tail can break off when grabbed, allowing the iguana to escape, and eventually grow a new one.

Going by their colour range, it's not surprising that Iguanas have very sharp colour vision, but they can also see ultraviolet wavelengths. In bright sunlight, they are also able to detect movement and shapes from a long distance, but their sight is much less effective in low light conditions.

If threatened, the Green Iguana's first response is to flee, preferably by diving into water. If cornered, it will extend the dewlap under its neck, hiss, bob its head, puff up its body, and lash out with claws and tail. Extending and displaying its dewlap is also used for more social behaviour to greet or court another Iguana.

DNA tests show that the iguana originated in South America and spread throughout Central America and the Caribbean. Partly as a result of their popularity as pets, they have been introduced to Grand Cayman, Puerto Rico, southern USA, Hawaii and the Virgin Islands where, too often, they were then released into the wild when their owners were unable to care for them properly. In 1995, Green Iguanas were washed ashore on the island of Anguilla after a hurricane and have since bred and colonised the island. Their ability to colonise, and their popularity as pets, has led the International Union for Conservation of Nature to recognise them as an invasive species, but one whose trade should be controlled in the interests of their long term future.

TOP: Females and juvenile male Green Iguanas are a much brighter green than adults. Juveniles stay in familial groups for the first year of their lives and, in the wild, the young males often use their own bodies to gallantly shield and protect their female siblings from predators.

BOTTOM: During cold weather, Green Iguanas prefer to stay on the ground for greater warmth. They can also regulate their body temperature through a prominent dewlap — a flap of skin hanging beneath their lower jaw. The dewlap is also used in courtships and territorial displays.

Bouquets and credits

While spending time at Taronga collating the material for this book, I couldn't resist the temptation to email or text my friends the occasional photo from my 'office window': a gorilla baby giggling with mum; a giraffe poking a long blue tongue up its own nose; a prolonged bear hug between the Sun Bears at the entrance to their private cave, almost as though they were seeing each other off at the start of a working day. It's been a dream project and I'd like to thank the people who made it possible: Sue Baker and Lisa Keen for their inspired vision, their unfailing enthusiasm and guidance at every hop, step and leap along the way.

Thank you to all the zoo keepers and curators who patiently fact-checked the details, and for the photographs they contributed from over many years with glimpses of their charges captured in unguarded moments.

An enormous thank you to the extremely talented professional photographers whom Taronga feels privileged to work with. This book would not have been possible without their patience during the infinite waits for that 'just right moment' across the decades of photographs we have been able to draw on. They are gratefully acknowledged by name below.

Thanks, too, to Jude Rowe of the Agave Creative Group for her, always, superb designs — it's the second Taronga book we've collaborated on; the first was *Life is a Zoo* also published by Citrus Press.

The paw prints at the beginning and end of this book were made by the animals themselves and it is a credit to their zoo carers that so many of them could be encouraged to contribute their inked imprints as a symbol of Taronga being 'For the Wild'. It's a vision which re-affirms Taronga's vital role in helping to achieve a shared future for wildlife and people, helping threatened species to breed, protecting their genetic diversity and even re-introducing them to the wild.

Catharine Retter, 2016.

Cover photographs
Tony Britt-Lewis, top left. Rick Stevens, top centre and top right. David Kirshner, bottom photo. Lorinda Taylor, back cover. Taronga, jacket flap.
Page i: Lorinda Taylor Page iii: Lorinda Taylor.

Introduction
Page 7: Rick Stevens

Page 87: Ben Gibson, top. Gary Ramage, bottom.

Page 89: Chris Kara.

Page 91: Rick Stevens, top. Paul Fahy, bottom.

Australasia

Page 92: Paul Fahy.

Page 95: Chloe Precey.

Page 97: Tony Britt-Lewis, top left. Chloe Precey, top right. Taronga, bottom.

Page 99: Lorinda Taylor

Page 100: Emma Lloyd, top. Lorinda Taylor, bottom.

Page 103: Rick Stevens

Page 105: Gary Ramage, top left and bottom right. Lorinda Taylor, top right.

Page 107: Taronga.

Page 108: Taronga, top left. Paul Fahy, top right. Tony Britt-Lewis, bottom.

Page 109: Paul Fahy.

Page 111: Rob Dockerill.

Page 113: Auspic, top. Lorinda Taylor, bottom.

Page 115: Taronga.

Page 117: Ellen Wilson, top left. Lorinda Taylor, top right. Tony Britt-Lewis, bottom.

Page 118: Taronga, top and bottom.

Page 121: Lorinda Taylor.

Page 123, 125: Rick Stevens.

Page 127: Taronga.

Page 128: Paul Fahy, top left and right. Rick Stevens, bottom.

Page 131: Taronga.

Page 133: Paul Fahy, top and bottom.

Page 135: Corrine Symons.

Page 137: Lorinda Taylor.

Page 138: Rick Stevens, top. Danielle Henry, bottom.

Page 141: Gary Ramage.

Page 143: Tony Britt-Lewis.

Page 145: Taronga, top left. Rick Stevens, top right, Taronga, bottom.

Page 147: Bobby-Jo Clow, top. Ben Gibson, bottom.

The Americas

Page 148: Paul Fahy.

Page 151: Taronga, top left and bottom. Paul Fahy, top right.

Page 153: Taronga.

Page 155: Lorinda Taylor.

Page 156: Lorinda Taylor, top. Gary Ramage, bottom.

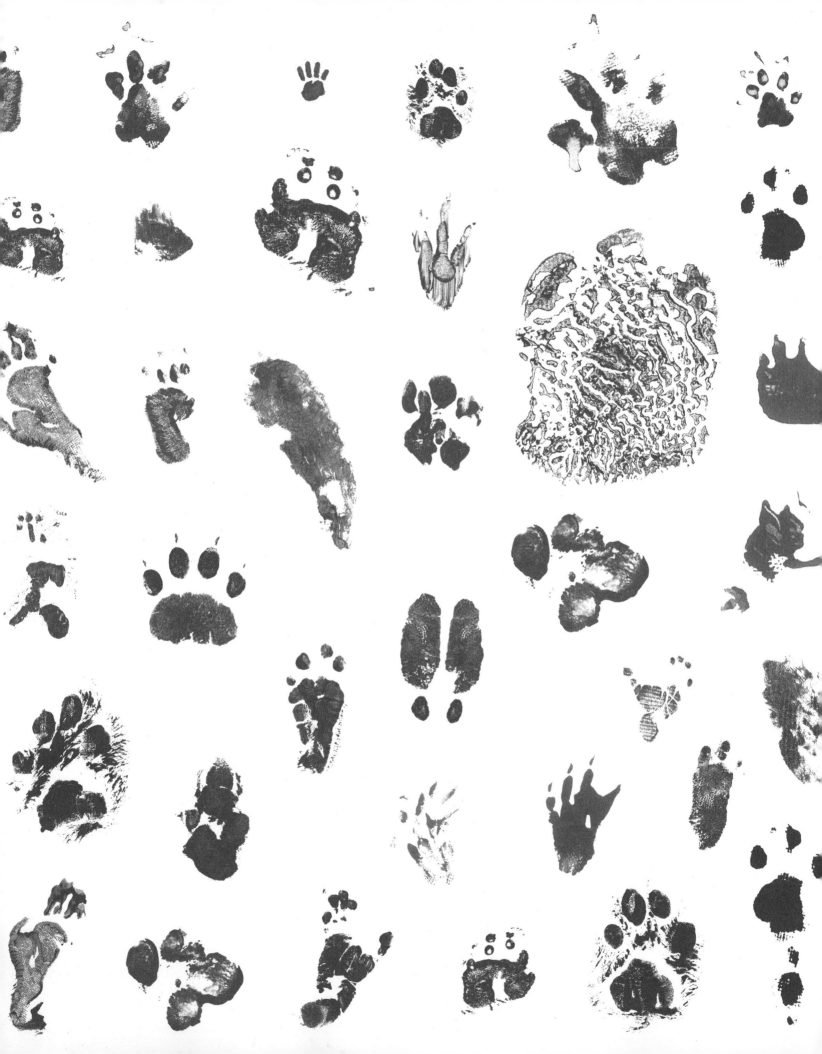